Handy Substitutions

Ingredient Needed	Substitute
Baking Products	
1 cup self-rising flour	1 cup all-purpose flour, 1 teaspoon baking powder, and ½ teaspoon salt
1 cup cake flour	1 cup minus 2 tablespoons all-purpose flour
1 cup all-purpose flour	1 cup plus 2 tablespoons cake flour
1 cup powdered sugar	1 cup sugar and 1 tablespoon cornstarch (processed in food processor)
1 cup honey	1¼ cups sugar and ¼ cup water
1 teaspoon baking powder	¼ teaspoon baking soda and ½ teaspoon cream of tartar
1 tablespoon cornstarch	2 tablespoons all-purpose flour
1 tablespoon tapioca	1½ tablespoons all-purpose flour
½ cup chopped pecans	½ cup regular oats, toasted (in baked products)
1 ounce or square unsweetened chocolate	3 tablespoons cocoa and 1 tablespoon butter or margarine
Eggs and Dairy Products	
2 large eggs	3 small eggs
1 cup fat-free milk	½ cup evaporated fat-free milk and ½ cup water
1 cup plain yogurt	1 cup buttermilk
1 cup fat-free sour cream	1 cup fat-free yogurt and 1 tablespoon cornstarch (for cooking)
Vegetable Products	
1 pound fresh mushrooms, sliced	1 (8-ounce) can sliced mushrooms, drained, or 3 ounces dried
1 medium onion, chopped	1 tablespoon instant minced onion or 1 tablespoon onion powder
3 tablespoons chopped shallots	2½ tablespoons chopped onion and 1 teaspoon chopped garlic
Seasoning Products	
1 tablespoon chopped fresh herbs	1 teaspoon dried herbs or ¼ teaspoon powdered herbs
1 garlic clove	⅛ teaspoon garlic powder or minced dried garlic or 1 teaspoon bottled minced garlic
1 tablespoon dried orange peel	1½ teaspoons orange extract or 1 tablespoon grated fresh orange rind
1 teaspoon ground allspice	½ teaspoon ground cinnamon and ½ teaspoon ground cloves
1 teaspoon pumpkin pie spice	½ teaspoon ground cinnamon, ¼ teaspoon ground ginger, ⅛ teaspoon ground allspice, and ⅛ teaspoon ground nutmeg
Alcohol	
2 tablespoons amaretto	¼ to ½ teaspoon almond extract
2 tablespoons dry sherry or bourbon	1 to 2 teaspoons vanilla extract
¼ cup Marsala	¼ cup dry white wine and 1 teaspoon brandy
¼ cup or more white wine	Equal measure of apple juice (in sweet dishes) or reduced-sodium chicken broth (in savory dishes)
¼ cup or more red wine	Equal measure of red grape juice or cranberry juice

Grouper Athenian
recipe, page 47

Skillet Ziti and
Vegetables
recipe, page 75

2

Balsamic Pork Chops
recipe, page 98

Roasted Asparagus
recipe, page 178

Pan-Glazed Chicken with Basil
recipe, page 105

Broccoli Couscous
recipe, page 186

Weight Watchers®

5 Ingredient
15 Minute
Cookbook

Oxmoor House®

© 2002 by Oxmoor House, Inc.
Book Division of Southern Progress Corporation
P.O. Box 2463, Birmingham, Alabama 35201

Library of Congress Control Number: 2002104062
ISBN: 0-8487-2525-5
Printed in the United States of America
Fourth Printing 2004

Be sure to check with your health-care provider before making any changes in your diet.

Editor-in-Chief: Nancy Fitzpatrick Wyatt
Executive Editor: Katherine M. Eakin
Art Director: Cynthia R. Cooper
Copy Chief: Catherine Ritter Scholl

Weight Watchers 5 Ingredient 15 Minute Cookbook

Editor: Carolyn Land, R.D.
Designer: Clare T. Minges
Copy Editor: Jacqueline Giovanelli
Editorial Assistant: Andrea B. Carver
Director, Test Kitchens: Elizabeth Tyler Luckett
Assistant Director, Test Kitchens: Julie Christopher
Recipe Editor: Gayle Hays Sadler
Test Kitchens Staff: Jennifer Cofield; Ana Kelly; Jan A. Smith
Senior Photographer: Jim Bathie
Photographer: Brit Huckabay
Senior Photo Stylist: Kay Clarke
Photo Stylist: Virginia R. Cravens
Publishing Systems Administrator: Rick Tucker
Director, Production and Distribution: Phillip Lee
Production Coordinator: Leslie Wells Johnson
Production Assistant: Faye Porter Bonner

Contributors:
Indexer: Mary Ann Laurens
Recipe Development: Karen Levin, Elizabeth Luckett, Carol H. Munson,
    OTT Communications, Elizabeth Taliaferro, Lisa H. Talley
Test Kitchens: Regan M. Jones, R.D.; Natalie E. King; Laurie V. Knowles;
    Kathleen Royal Phillips; Kate M. Wheeler, R.D.

Cover: Buenos Burritos, page 111, and Mexican Corn Salad, page 141

To order additional publications,
call 1-800-765-6400.

For more books to enrich your life, visit
oxmoorhouse.com

Contents

Introduction

Seven Suppertime Solutions 8

How to Use These Recipes 10

Recipes

Breads 11

Desserts......................................19

Fish & Shellfish 39

Meatless Main Dishes 65

Meats......................................79

Poultry 103

Salads......................................129

Sandwiches...............................145

Soups 161

Vegetables & Side Dishes 177

Recipe Index..................................189

75% of Americans don't know at 4 p.m. what they'll eat for dinner, but whatever it is had better be healthy, tasty, and fast.

Seven 7 Suppertime* Solutions

How do you get a quick, low-***POINT*** dinner on the table that the whole family will love? Let *Weight Watchers® 5 Ingredient 15 Minute Cookbook* show you the way. You'll learn how to simplify your grocery shopping, put together delicious, wholesome meals using easy recipes, and stay within your ***POINTS*** range.

With each turn of the page, you'll find a meal that fits into your busy schedule and satisfies your family's taste buds. Since each recipe uses on average 5 ingredients, but never more than 10—not including salt, pepper, water, and cooking spray—it won't take much time to make a meal. Some recipes, like **Chicken Alfredo Pasta (page 122),** use just 5 ingredients; others may have more than 5 ingredients but take 15 minutes or less to prepare, such as **Ground Beef Stroganoff (page 86);** and some can be made in 15 minutes with just 5 ingredients like **Mediterranean Pasta with Zucchini (page 73).** Now you'll always have the answer when you hear the question, "What's for dinner?".

Below are seven suggestions that will help put *Weight Watchers® 5 Ingredient 15 Minute Cookbook* to work for you.

1. Plan Ahead.

- Plan meals at the beginning of the week before the rush begins.
- As you plan, make use of the **No-Stress Shopping List** located on the inside front cover of the book. This list includes the basic ingredients you'll need to make more than a third of the recipes. Many of the recipes use the same pantry staples and frozen ingredients, so you'll always have food items on hand when you need to put together a fast meal.

- Check out new convenience products, such as the bagged produce that's already washed and chopped for you.
- Arrange the ingredients for the next evening's meal in the fridge or freezer or on the counter the night before.

2. Don't Worry!

Sure, **Teriyaki-Ginger Pork Tenderloin (page 94)** sounds delicious, but you need an *entire* meal! That's why we've given you suggestions for side dishes below each main-dish recipe. Once you've picked your entrée, look for the **Serve with** box just below it. This box will refer you to a quick-fix side dish recipe in the book or will suggest on-hand commercial products to round out the meal.

3. Get the Facts.

To help you manage your time in the kitchen, we give you either **work time** and **cook time** or **total time.** When the preparation and the cooking time are two distinct steps, we give you the work time and the cook time. The work time is never more than 15 minutes, but there may be some cook time—like with a slow cooker recipe—during which you could be doing something else.

4. Slow Down to Speed Up.

Learn how to let a slow cooker do the work for you! How does delicious **Glazed Turkey (page 127),** succulent **Italian Pot Roast (page 91),** or low-*POINT* **Chili Grande (page 167)** sound for dinner? These recipes have 6 ingredients or less and cook on their own while you do other things. Set aside a few minutes in the morning to set up your slow cooker, and you've got a mouth-watering meal waiting when you walk in the door.

5. Avoid the Rush Hour.

On those extra-busy days, try these recipes that guarantee dinner on the table in *less than 15 minutes*: **Roasted Garlic-Potato Soup (page 162), Orange-Glazed Salmon (page 50),** or **Tortellini Primavera with Pesto Sauce (page 74).**

6. Lose Weight on the *POINTS* Plan.

Running low on *POINTS* at the end of the day? Then you'll love these low-*POINT* dishes. Try **Sweet-and-Sour Shrimp (page 58), Honey-Mustard Pork with Wilted Spinach (page 95),** or **Tuscan Chicken and Beans (page 107)**—they're only 3 *POINTS* per serving. And, don't miss the tasty 2-*POINT* **Sausage and Black Bean Soup (page 172).**

Every recipe in this book fits easily into the Weight Watchers **Winning Points** plan. In addition, meals contain no more than 30% calories from fat, according to the current dietary recommendations. Plus, we suggest a variety of fresh fruits and vegetables, whole grain breads, and low-fat dairy products that add extra fiber and calcium to your diet and take the guesswork out of healthy eating. As an added bonus, each recipe has the nutrient information, *POINTS*, and exchange values for one serving so you can keep track and stay on track. (For more information, see **How to Use These Recipes on page 10.**)

7. Get Started!

What are you waiting for? You have more than 90 quick Weight Watchers meals at your fingertips. That's enough for three months, or one-fourth of the year!

How to Use These Recipes

Weight Watchers® 5 Ingredient 15 Minute Cookbook gives you the nutrition facts you need. To make your life easier, we've provided the following useful information with every recipe:

- A number calculated through **POINTS®** Food System, an integral part of the **Winning Points®** Weight-Loss System from Weight Watchers International, Inc.
- Diabetic exchange values for those who use them as a guide for planning meals
- A complete nutrient analysis per serving

POINTS Food System

Every recipe in the book includes a number assigned through **POINTS** value. This system uses a formula based on the calorie, fat, and fiber content of the food. Foods with more calories and fat (like a slice of pepperoni pizza) receive high numbers, while fruits and vegetables receive low numbers. For more information about the **Winning Points** Weight-Loss System and the Weight Watchers meeting nearest you, call 1-800-651-6000.

Diabetic Exchanges

Exchange values are provided for people who use them for calorie-controlled diets and for people with diabetes. All foods within a certain group contain approximately the same amount of nutrients and calories, so one serving of a food from a food group can be substituted or exchanged for one serving of any other item on the list. The food groups are meat, starch, vegetable, fruit, fat, and milk. The exchange values are based on the Exchange Lists for Meal Planning developed by the American Diabetes Association and the American Dietetic Association.

Nutritional Analyses

Each recipe has a complete list of nutrients; the nutritional analyses are based on these assumptions:

- Unless otherwise indicated, meat, poultry, and fish refer to skinned, boned, and cooked servings.
- When we give a range for an ingredient (3 to 3½ cups flour, for instance), we calculate using the lesser amount.
- Some alcohol calories evaporate during heating; the analysis reflects that.
- Only the amount of marinade absorbed by the food is used in calculation.
- Garnishes and optional ingredients are not included in the analysis.

The nutritional values used in our calculations either come from a computer program or are provided by food manufacturers.

breads

total time ❋ 12 minutes

Garlic Bread

POINTS:

2

1   (6-ounce) loaf French bread
Olive oil-flavored cooking spray
1   tablespoon minced garlic

exchanges:

1½ Starch

1. Preheat oven to 350°.

2. Slice loaf into 4 slices, and coat each slice with cooking spray. Spread garlic evenly over slices. Wrap loaf in aluminum foil, and bake at 350° for 10 minutes or until thoroughly heated. Yield: 4 slices.

per slice: Calories 129; Carbohydrate 24.3g; Fat 1.1g (saturated 0.3g); Fiber 1.0g; Protein 4.0g; Cholesterol 1mg; Sodium 247mg; Calcium 36mg; Iron 1.1mg

total time ❋ 6 minutes

Parmesan Toasts

POINTS:

2

4   (1-ounce) slices Italian bread
Olive oil-flavored cooking spray
¼   teaspoon freshly ground black pepper
4   teaspoons grated Parmesan cheese

exchanges:

1 Starch

1. Preheat broiler.

2. Coat slices with cooking spray; sprinkle evenly with pepper. Top each slice with cheese, and broil until lightly browned. Yield: 4 servings.

per slice: Calories 93; Carbohydrate 17.1g; Fat 1.0g (saturated 0.3g); Fiber 0.8g; Protein 3.4g; Cholesterol 2mg; Sodium 207mg; Calcium 30mg; Iron 0.9mg

Garlic-Cheese Breadsticks

¼ cup (1 ounce) grated Parmesan cheese
¼ teaspoon garlic powder
1 (11-ounce) can refrigerated soft breadstick dough

1. Combine cheese and garlic powder. Prepare breadsticks according to package directions, pressing each stick into cheese mixture before baking. Yield: 8 breadsticks.

per breadstick: Calories 122; Carbohydrate 19.2g; Fat 2.8g (saturated 0.5g); Fiber 0.5g; Protein 2.6g; Cholesterol 2mg; Sodium 337mg; Calcium 43mg; Iron 1.0mg

POINTS:
3

exchanges:
1 Starch
½ Fat

Pretzel Breadsticks

Quickly twist ordinary breadsticks into a fun pretzel shape. If you don't mind a little extra sodium, lightly sprinkle the pretzels with salt before baking.

1 (7-ounce) can refrigerated breadstick dough
Butter-flavored cooking spray

1. Prepare breadsticks according to package directions, coating with cooking spray before baking. Shape each breadstick into a pretzel shape before baking. Yield: 5 breadsticks.

per breadstick: Calories 110; Carbohydrate 18.0g; Fat 2.5g (saturated 0.5g); Fiber 0.5g; Protein 3.0g; Cholesterol 0mg; Sodium 290mg; Calcium 0mg; Iron 0mg

POINTS:
2

exchanges:
1 Starch
½ Fat

Garlic-Dill Rolls

POINTS:
2

exchanges:
1 Starch
½ Fat

1 (11.3-ounce) can refrigerated roll dough
1½ tablespoons light mayonnaise
2 teaspoons dried dill
¼ teaspoon garlic powder

1. Preheat oven to 375°.

2. Place rolls on a baking sheet according to package directions. Combine mayonnaise, dill, and garlic powder in a small bowl. Brush mayonnaise mixture evenly over rolls, and bake at 375° for 15 minutes or until golden. Yield: 8 rolls.

per roll: Calories 118; Carbohydrate 18.3g; Fat 2.8g (saturated 0.1g); Fiber 0.5g; Protein 4.6g; Cholesterol 1mg; Sodium 291mg; Calcium 5mg; Iron 1.2mg

Chili-Onion Drop Biscuits

POINTS:
2

exchanges:
1 Starch

1 cup low-fat baking mix (such as reduced-fat Bisquick)
⅓ cup fat-free milk
2 green onions, chopped
1 teaspoon chili powder
Cooking spray

1. Preheat oven to 450°.

2. Combine baking mix, milk, onions, and chili powder in a bowl; stir just until dry ingredients are moistened. Drop dough onto a baking sheet coated with cooking spray. Bake at 450° for 7 minutes or until golden. Yield: 6 biscuits.

per biscuit: Calories 83; Carbohydrate 15.3g; Fat 1.4g (saturated 0.3g); Fiber 0.5g; Protein 2.1g; Cholesterol 0mg; Sodium 242mg; Calcium 38mg; Iron 0.8mg

work time: 3 minutes ❋ **cook time:** 16 minutes

Skillet Corn Bread
photo, page 62

1   (7.5-ounce) package yellow corn muffin mix
½   cup water
Cooking spray

1. Preheat oven to 400°.

2. Prepare muffin mix according to package directions using ½ cup water. Pour batter into an 8-inch ovenproof skillet coated with cooking spray, and bake at 400° for 16 minutes or until golden. Cut into wedges. Yield: 6 wedges.

per wedge: Calories 133; Carbohydrate 25.8g; Fat 2.9g (saturated 0.8g); Fiber 0.4g; Protein 1.7g; Cholesterol 0mg; Sodium 233mg; Calcium 68mg; Iron 0.9mg

POINTS:
3

exchanges:
1½ Starch
½ Fat

---

total time ❋ 10 minutes

Bagel Chips

These chips are a great accompaniment to sandwiches, salads, soups, and dips. Add variety by substituting your favorite flavored bagel for the plain.

2   (2¼-ounce) plain bagels
Butter-flavored cooking spray

1. Preheat oven to 350°.

2. Slice bagels into thin slices, using a serrated knife. Coat slices with cooking spray. Bake at 350° for 5 minutes or until crisp. Yield: 4 servings.

per serving: Calories 84; Carbohydrate 17.2g; Fat 0.5g (saturated 0.0g); Fiber 1.0g; Protein 3.1g; Cholesterol 0mg; Sodium 145mg; Calcium 4mg; Iron 1.0mg

POINTS:
2

exchanges:
1 Starch

Toasted Pita Chips

POINTS: 3   (6-inch) pitas
1   Butter-flavored cooking spray

exchanges:
1 Starch

1. Preheat oven to 400°.

2. Split pitas in half horizontally. Cut each half into 8 wedges. Arrange wedges, rough sides up, on a baking sheet, and generously coat with cooking spray. Bake at 400° for 6 to 7 minutes or until crisp and golden. Yield: 6 servings (serving size: 8 wedges).

per serving: Calories 77; Carbohydrate 14.1g; Fat 0.9g (saturated 0.0g); Fiber 2.6g; Protein 1.4g; Cholesterol 0mg; Sodium 349mg; Calcium 26mg; Iron 0.8mg

Zesty Pita Wedges

POINTS: 2   (6-inch) pitas
1   1   teaspoon Greek seasoning
Olive oil-flavored cooking spray

exchanges:
1 Starch

1. Preheat oven to 400°.

2. Split pitas in half horizontally. Cut each half into 8 wedges. Arrange wedges, rough sides up, on a baking sheet. Generously coat wedges with cooking spray, and sprinkle with Greek seasoning. Bake at 400° for 6 to 7 minutes or until crisp. Yield: 4 servings (serving size: 8 wedges).

per serving: Calories 77; Carbohydrate 14.1g; Fat 0.9g (saturated 0.0g); Fiber 2.6g; Protein 1.4g; Cholesterol 0mg; Sodium 349mg; Calcium 26mg; Iron 0.8mg

total time ❋ 8 minutes

Tortilla Wedges

To add a flavor punch, lightly sprinkle the wedges with a dried herb or garlic salt after coating them with cooking spray.

4   (8-inch) flour tortillas
Butter-flavored cooking spray

1. Preheat oven to 400°.

2. Cut tortillas into wedges, and coat with cooking spray. Bake at 400° for 4 to 5 minutes or until lightly browned and crisp. Yield: 4 servings (serving size: 4 wedges).

per serving: Calories 140; Carbohydrate 23.6g; Fat 3.2g (saturated 0.5g); Fiber 1.3g; Protein 3.7g; Cholesterol 0mg; Sodium 203mg; Calcium 97mg; Iron 1.0mg

POINTS:
3

exchanges:
1½ Starch
½ Fat

---

total time ❋ 12 minutes (about 2 minutes per bowl)

Tortilla Bowls

These bowls are super-easy to make and ideal for holding chili, soup, or salad.

6   (10-inch) flour tortillas

1. For each tortilla bowl, line a 1½-quart glass bowl with 1 tortilla. Prick holes in the bottom of tortilla with a fork. Microwave at HIGH 2 to 3 minutes or until crisp. Remove from oven, and let cool slightly in glass bowl. Remove tortilla from bowl. Repeat process for remaining tortillas. Place tortilla bowl in a shallow dish; spoon chili or salad into tortilla bowl. Yield: 6 bowls (serving size: 1 bowl).

per bowl: Calories 161; Carbohydrate 27.6g; Fat 3.5g (saturated 0.6g); Fiber 1.5g; Protein 4.3g; Cholesterol 0mg; Sodium 237mg; Calcium 38mg; Iron 0.9mg

POINTS:
3

exchanges:
2 Starch

Baked Won Ton Crisps photo, page 43

POINTS:

2

exchanges:

1 Starch

½ Fat

1½ teaspoons sesame or vegetable oil

1½ teaspoons water

12 won ton wrappers

1½ teaspoons sesame seeds

¼ teaspoon salt

1. Preheat oven to 400°.

2. Combine oil and water; brush evenly over won tons. Sprinkle sesame seeds and salt evenly over won tons. Bake at 400° for 5 minutes or until lightly browned and crisp. Yield: 4 servings (serving size: 3 crisps).

per serving: Calories 79; Carbohydrate 11.7g; Fat 2.6g (saturated 0.4g); Fiber 0.1g; Protein 2.1g; Cholesterol 2mg; Sodium 260mg; Calcium 13mg; Iron 0.9mg

Cinnamon Waffle Crisps

POINTS:

1

exchanges:

1 Starch

1 tablespoon sugar

¼ teaspoon ground cinnamon

2 frozen waffles

Butter-flavored cooking spray

1. Preheat oven to 450°.

2. Combine sugar and cinnamon, stirring well. Coat frozen waffles with cooking spray, and sprinkle each with ½ tablespoon sugar mixture. Place on a baking sheet; bake at 450° for 5 to 7 minutes or until crisp. Cut each waffle into 4 wedges. Yield: 4 servings (serving size: 2 wedges).

per serving: Calories 59; Carbohydrate 12.0g; Fat 0.8g (saturated 0.1g); Fiber 0.3g; Protein 1.5g; Cholesterol 6mg; Sodium 80mg; Calcium 12mg; Iron 1.0mg

desserts

Raspberry-Lemon Parfaits photo, facing page

Bright red raspberries turn a simple carton of yogurt into an elegant ending to dinner.

POINTS:

2

exchanges:

1 Starch

½ Fruit

2   cups raspberries

2   (8-ounce) cartons lemon low-fat yogurt

1. Layer raspberries and yogurt evenly into 4 (6-ounce) parfait glasses, beginning and ending with raspberries. Yield: 4 servings.

per serving: Calories 127; Carbohydrate 22.8g; Fat 1.8g (saturated 0.9g); Fiber 4.2g; Protein 6.2g; Cholesterol 6mg; Sodium 74mg; Calcium 208mg; Iron 0.4mg

Refreshing Melon Duo

The balsamic vinegar brightens the mild flavors of the melons.

POINTS:

1

exchanges:

1 Fruit

2   cups cubed honeydew melon

2   cups cubed cantaloupe

¼   cup white balsamic vinegar

1   teaspoon brown sugar

1. Combine honeydew and cantaloupe in a bowl. Combine balsamic vinegar and brown sugar; stir to dissolve. Pour over melon cubes; stir gently to coat. Cover and chill until ready to serve. Yield: 4 (1-cup) servings.

per serving: Calories 62; Carbohydrate 15.9g; Fat 0.3g (saturated 0.2g); Fiber 1.7g; Protein 1.1g; Cholesterol 0mg; Sodium 16mg; Calcium 20mg; Iron 0.4mg

**Raspberry-Lemon
Parfaits**
recipe, facing page

21

Chocolate-Peanut Butter Pie
recipe, page 35

Ice Cream Sandwiches
recipe, page 33

Chocolate Chip Frozen Yogurt
recipe, facing page

total time ❋ 3 minutes

Chocolate Chip Frozen Yogurt photo, facing page

Kids love to help in the kitchen, so let them stir the chips into this sweet treat.

½   cup chocolate chips
2   cups vanilla low-fat frozen yogurt, softened

POINTS:
4

1. Stir chocolate chips into frozen yogurt. Spoon into 4 dessert dishes. Yield: 4 (½-cup) servings.

exchanges:
2½ Starch
1 Fat

per serving: Calories 196; Carbohydrate 36.7g; Fat 4.0g (saturated 4.0g); Fiber 0.0g; Protein 4.2g; Cholesterol 0mg; Sodium 56mg; Calcium 107mg; Iron 0.7mg

total time ❋ 7 minutes

Strawberries and Cream

Almond extract enhances the sweetness of the berries.

4   cups sliced strawberries
2   teaspoons sugar
1½ cups frozen reduced-calorie whipped topping, thawed
½   teaspoon almond extract

POINTS:
1

exchanges:
1 Fruit
½ Fat

1. Sprinkle sugar over strawberries. Combine whipped topping and almond extract. Spoon strawberries evenly into 6 dessert dishes. Top evenly with whipped topping. Yield: 6 servings.

per serving: Calories 72; Carbohydrate 12.2g; Fat 2.5g (saturated 0.0g); Fiber 2.6g; Protein 1.1g; Cholesterol 0mg; Sodium 13mg; Calcium 16mg; Iron 0.4mg

Cinnamon-Apple Yogurt

Make your own cinnamon-sugar by combining ½ teaspoon cinnamon with 3½ teaspoons sugar. If you like more cinnamon flavor, increase the cinnamon.

POINTS:
2

exchanges:
1 Starch
½ Skim Milk

2 cups vanilla low-fat frozen yogurt
½ cup unsweetened applesauce
4 teaspoons bottled cinnamon-sugar

1. Spoon ½ cup yogurt into each of 4 dessert dishes. Top each serving with 2 tablespoons applesauce and 1 teaspoon cinnamon-sugar. Yield: 4 servings.

per serving: Calories 114; Carbohydrate 20.4g; Fat 1.5g (saturated 0.9g); Fiber 0.5g; Protein 5.7g; Cholesterol 6mg; Sodium 76mg; Calcium 108mg; Iron 0.3mg

Mocha Milkshake

To heighten your chocolate experience, substitute chocolate ice cream for the vanilla.

POINTS:
4

exchanges:
2½ Starch
1 Fat

3¼ cups vanilla low-fat ice cream
¾ cup cold coffee
¼ cup fat-free hot fudge topping
1½ cups ice

1. Combine vanilla ice cream, cold coffee, hot fudge topping, and ice in container of an electric blender; cover and process until smooth. Yield: 4 (1-cup) servings.

per serving: Calories 195; Carbohydrate 36.0g; Fat 4.6g (saturated 2.8g); Fiber 1.0g; Protein 5.1g; Cholesterol 15mg; Sodium 138mg; Calcium 193mg; Iron 0.9mg

Raspberry Smoothies

This cool, refreshing beverage is a perfect after-workout rejuvenator.

1   (8-ounce) carton lemon low-fat yogurt
1½ cups frozen reduced-calorie whipped topping, thawed
1½ cups raspberries
5   ice cubes

POINTS:

2

exchanges:
1 Starch
1 Fruit

1. Combine yogurt, whipped topping, raspberries, and ice cubes in container of an electric blender; cover and process until smooth. Yield: 4 (1-cup) servings.

per serving: Calories 144; Carbohydrate 30.8g; Fat 0.7g (saturated 0.0g); Fiber 3.1g; Protein 2.5g; Cholesterol 0mg; Sodium 52mg; Calcium 107mg; Iron 0.3mg

Honeybee Sundaes

If you have extra time, lightly toast the almonds for a richer, nuttier flavor.

2   cups vanilla low-fat frozen yogurt
4   tablespoons honey
4   teaspoons sliced almonds

POINTS:

3

exchanges:
2 Starch
½ Fat

1. Spoon ½ cup yogurt into each of 4 dessert dishes. Drizzle each serving with 1 tablespoon honey and sprinkle with 1 teaspoon sliced almonds. Yield: 4 servings.

per serving: Calories 159; Carbohydrate 32.3g; Fat 3.0g (saturated 1.3g); Fiber 0.3g; Protein 3.0g; Cholesterol 8mg; Sodium 29mg; Calcium 106mg; Iron 0.2mg

Berries and Cream

The honey adds just the right amount of sweetness to this dessert.

POINTS:
1

2   cups blueberries
2   cups quartered strawberries
½   cup vanilla low-fat frozen yogurt, slightly softened

exchanges:
2 Fruit

1½ tablespoons honey

1. Combine blueberries and strawberries; spoon into 4 dessert dishes. Combine yogurt and honey; spoon evenly over fruit mixture. Yield: 4 (1-cup) servings.

per serving: Calories 111; Carbohydrate 26.0g; Fat 0.9g (saturated 0.3g); Fiber 5.2g; Protein 2.4g; Cholesterol 1mg; Sodium 24mg; Calcium 41mg; Iron 0.5mg

Fruited Frozen Yogurt

Shhh! Don't tell anyone, but this frozen treat is a great source of calcium.

POINTS:
2

1   (8-ounce) can crushed pineapple, drained
2   cups vanilla fat-free frozen yogurt, slightly softened

exchanges:
1 Starch
1 Fruit

1. Stir pineapple into frozen yogurt. Spoon into 4 dessert dishes. Yield: 4 (½-cup) servings.

per serving: Calories 113; Carbohydrate 25.4g; Fat 0.0g (saturated 0.0g); Fiber 0.3g; Protein 3.2g; Cholesterol 3mg; Sodium 50mg; Calcium 106mg; Iron 0.2mg

Layered Waffle-Fruit Cup

Think waffles are only for breakfast? Not anymore!

1	cup chopped strawberries
½	cup crushed pineapple, drained
1	cup vanilla fat-free frozen yogurt
4	fat-free frozen waffles, toasted and torn into small pieces

POINTS:
3

exchanges:
1 Starch
1 Fruit

1. Combine strawberries, pineapple, and yogurt.

2. Divide half of waffle pieces among 4 parfait glasses. Spoon ⅓ cup yogurt mixture over waffle pieces in each glass. Repeat procedure with remaining half of waffle pieces and yogurt mixture. Yield: 4 servings.

per serving: Calories 149; Carbohydrate 30.9g; Fat 1.5g (saturated 0.3g); Fiber 1.6g; Protein 4.9g; Cholesterol 13mg; Sodium 189mg; Calcium 80mg; Iron 2.1mg

Strawberry Sundaes

You can enjoy this fruit dessert year-round by substituting unsweetened frozen strawberries for the fresh.

2	cups sliced strawberries
2	cups vanilla fat-free frozen yogurt
	Strawberry slices (optional)

POINTS:
2

exchanges:
1 Starch
1 Fruit

1. Place strawberries in a blender; process until smooth. Spoon ½ cup frozen yogurt into each of 4 bowls. Spoon strawberry puree evenly over yogurt. Garnish with additional strawberry slices, if desired. Yield: 4 servings.

per serving: Calories 125; Carbohydrate 27.8g; Fat 0.3g (saturated 0.0g); Fiber 1.9g; Protein 3.5g; Cholesterol 3mg; Sodium 51mg; Calcium 112mg; Iron 0.3mg

Neapolitan Sundaes

POINTS:

4

exchanges:
2 Starch
½ Fruit
½ Fat

1   cup sliced strawberries
¼   cup chocolate chips
4   (1-ounce) slices angel food cake
1⅓ cups vanilla low-fat frozen yogurt

1. Place strawberries in a blender; process until smooth. Place chocolate chips in a small zip-top plastic bag, and crush with a meat mallet or rolling pin. Drizzle strawberry puree evenly on 4 plates, and place cake slices on top of puree. Top each cake slice with ⅓ cup frozen yogurt, and sprinkle each with 1 tablespoon crushed chocolate chips. Yield: 4 servings.

per serving: Calories 193; Carbohydrate 40.1g; Fat 2.2g (saturated 2.0g); Fiber 0.9g; Protein 4.5g; Cholesterol 0mg; Sodium 181mg; Calcium 115mg; Iron 0.6mg

Caramel-Banana Sundaes

POINTS:

4

exchanges:
2 Starch
1 Fruit

⅓   cup firmly packed brown sugar
1   tablespoon water
2   large bananas, peeled and sliced
2   cups vanilla fat-free ice cream
4   teaspoons fat-free caramel topping

1. Combine brown sugar and water in a large nonstick skillet. Cook over medium heat until sugar melts. Add bananas to skillet; cook over low heat 2 minutes or until banana is heated. Spoon banana mixture evenly over ½-cup portions of ice cream; top each serving with 1 teaspoon fat-free caramel topping. Yield: 4 servings.

per serving: Calories 207; Carbohydrate 49.0g; Fat 0.2g (saturated 0.1g); Fiber 1.3g; Protein 2.5g; Cholesterol 0mg; Sodium 60mg; Calcium 76mg; Iron 0.5mg

Caramel-Toffee Parfaits

1   large banana, peeled, cut in half, and halved lengthwise
2   cups vanilla fat-free ice cream
2   tablespoons plus 2 teaspoons fat-free caramel topping
1   (1.4-ounce) chocolate toffee crisp bar, finely chopped

POINTS:
5

exchanges:
3 Starch
½ Fat

1. Place 1 banana piece in each of 4 (4-ounce) parfait glasses or small bowls. Spoon ¼ cup ice cream onto each banana piece; top each with 1 teaspoon caramel topping. Sprinkle half of crushed candy evenly over parfaits. Repeat layers beginning with ice cream. Serve immediately. Yield: 4 servings.

per serving: Calories 223; Carbohydrate 45.0g; Fat 3.6g (saturated 2.2g); Fiber 1.0g; Protein 4.1g; Cholesterol 5mg; Sodium 109mg; Calcium 102mg; Iron 0.2mg

Chocolate-Peppermint Parfaits

⅓   cup finely crushed hard peppermint candies (about 11 candies)
2¼ cups frozen fat-free whipped topping, thawed
4   (3.5-ounce) containers prepared chocolate fat-free pudding

POINTS:
3

exchanges:
2½ Starch

1. Set aside 1 tablespoon crushed candies. Fold remaining crushed candies into whipped topping; set aside ½ cup topping mixture. Spoon half of remaining whipped topping mixture evenly into 4 parfait glasses. Layer half of each pudding cup evenly over topping mixture in glasses. Repeat layers.

2. Top each parfait with 2 tablespoons reserved topping mixture; sprinkle evenly with reserved tablespoon crushed candies. Yield: 4 servings.

per serving: Calories 167; Carbohydrate 37.5g; Fat 0.3g (saturated 0.2g); Fiber 0.6g; Protein 2.0g; Cholesterol 2mg; Sodium 157mg; Calcium 63mg; Iron 0.4mg

Strawberry-Waffle Shortcakes

This dessert is inspired by the traditionally heavy, rich Belgian waffles.

POINTS:

2

exchanges:

1 Starch

1 Fruit

2 cups sliced strawberries

4 fat-free frozen waffles, toasted

½ cup strawberry fat-free frozen yogurt, slightly softened

1. Spoon ½ cup sliced strawberries over each waffle; top each with 2 tablespoons frozen yogurt. Yield: 4 servings.

per serving: Calories 132; Carbohydrate 27.0g; Fat 1.5g (saturated 0.3g); Fiber 2.3g; Protein 4.3g; Cholesterol 13mg; Sodium 175mg; Calcium 69mg; Iron 2.1mg

Wafflewiches

It's best to eat these chocolate sandwiches with a fork and knife.

POINTS:

3

exchanges:

2 Starch

1 cup chocolate fat-free frozen yogurt, slightly softened

4 fat-free frozen waffles, toasted

2 tablespoons fat-free chocolate syrup

1. Spread ½ cup softened frozen yogurt over each of 2 toasted waffles. Top with remaining 2 toasted waffles. Cut each wafflewich into 4 wedges, and drizzle 2 tablespoons chocolate sauce evenly over wedges. Yield: 4 servings (serving size: 2 wedges).

per serving: Calories 152; Carbohydrate 31.4g; Fat 1.4g (saturated 0.3g); Fiber 0.5g; Protein 4.9g; Cholesterol 13mg; Sodium 194mg; Calcium 72mg; Iron 2.0mg

Strawberry Whip Parfaits

Soft bites of cake soak up the lighter-than-air strawberry cream.

2   cups sliced strawberries
2   cups fat-free frozen whipped topping, thawed
4   (1-ounce) slices angel food cake

1. Place strawberries in blender; process until smooth, stopping once to scrape down sides. Fold strawberry puree into whipped topping.

2. Tear angel food cake into pieces, and fold into strawberry mixture. Spoon evenly into 4 parfait glasses; cover and chill 30 minutes. Yield: 4 servings.

per serving: Calories 155; Carbohydrate 33.9g; Fat 0.4g (saturated 0.0g); Fiber 1.9g; Protein 2.2g; Cholesterol 0mg; Sodium 165mg; Calcium 51mg; Iron 0.5mg

POINTS:
3

exchanges:
1 Starch
1 Fruit

Ice Cream Sandwiches photo, page 23

These 2-*POINT* frozen treats are hard to resist no matter what flavor of ice cream you use.

1½ cups chocolate or vanilla fat-free ice cream, softened
16   chocolate wafer cookies

1. Spread 3 tablespoons ice cream onto flat side of 1 wafer cookie, and top with 1 wafer cookie. Wrap each sandwich in heavy-duty plastic wrap, and store in freezer. Yield: 8 servings (serving size: 1 sandwich).

per serving: Calories 94; Carbohydrate 18.2g; Fat 1.6g (saturated 0.6g); Fiber 0.4g; Protein 1.9g; Cholesterol 1mg; Sodium 109mg; Calcium 30mg; Iron 0.4mg

POINTS:
2

exchanges:
1 Starch

Frozen Raspberry Desserts

**This quick, throw-together dessert can be made ahead
and pulled out of the freezer for last-minute entertaining.**

POINTS:

2

1

exchanges:

½ Fruit

2   (3.5-ounce) cartons vanilla fat-free pudding

1   cup frozen reduced-calorie whipped topping, thawed

½   cup raspberries

1. Line 8 muffin cups with paper muffin liners. Fold together vanilla pudding, whipped topping, and raspberries. Divide mixture evenly, among muffin cups; cover and freeze at least 2 hours. Yield: 8 servings.

per serving: Calories 39; Carbohydrate 8.4g; Fat 0.0g (saturated 0.0g); Fiber 0.6g; Protein 0.6g; Cholesterol 0mg; Sodium 43mg; Calcium 21mg; Iron 0.1mg

Frozen Chocolate Pie

POINTS:

2

exchanges:

1½ Starch

Cooking spray

13   chocolate wafer cookies

3   cups chocolate fat-free no-sugar-added ice cream, slightly softened

1. Coat a 9-inch pie plate with cooking spray. Coarsely crush 8 wafer cookies; press crumbs into bottom of pie plate, and set aside. Spoon ice cream over prepared crumbs. Top ice cream with 5 additional crushed wafer cookies; cover and freeze 2 hours or until firm. To serve, cut into wedges. Yield: 8 servings.

per serving: Calories 117; Carbohydrate 23.6g; Fat 1.4g (saturated 0.4g); Fiber 1.1g; Protein 3.6g; Cholesterol 0mg; Sodium 102mg; Calcium 63mg; Iron 0.7mg

Chocolate-Peanut Butter Pie photo, page 22

¾ cup nutlike cereal nuggets (such as Grape-Nuts), divided
2   cups chocolate low-fat ice cream, slightly softened
1   (2.1-ounce) package sugar-free chocolate instant pudding mix
¼ cup creamy peanut butter
1   cup frozen fat-free whipped topping, thawed

POINTS:

4

exchanges:
2 Starch
1 Fat

1. Sprinkle ½ cup cereal nuggets evenly in bottom of an 8-inch round cake pan. Combine remaining ¼ cup cereal nuggets, ice cream, pudding mix, and peanut butter in a bowl. Fold in 1 cup whipped topping. Spoon mixture into prepared pan; cover and freeze 2 hours or until firm. Let stand at room temperature 15 minutes before serving. Yield: 8 servings.

per serving: Calories 177; Carbohydrate 28g; Fat 5g (saturated 1.7g); Fiber 2g; Protein 5g; Cholesterol 5mg; Sodium 386mg; Calcium 47mg; Iron 1.1mg

Strawberry Shortcakes

Enjoy a classic summer favorite for only 2 *POINTS*.

4   (1-ounce) slices angel food cake
2   cups sliced strawberries
1   cup frozen reduced-calorie whipped topping, thawed

POINTS:

2

exchanges:
1 Starch
1 Fruit

1. Place 1 cake slice on each of 4 plates. Top each slice with ½ cup sliced strawberries and ¼ cup whipped topping. Yield: 4 servings.

per serving: Calories 125; Carbohydrate 27.9g; Fat 0.4g (saturated 0.0g); Fiber 1.9g; Protein 2.2g; Cholesterol 0mg; Sodium 155mg; Calcium 51mg; Iron 0.5mg

Raspberry Shortcakes

With the help of prepared cake, this dessert is a snap to assemble.

POINTS:
3

½ (16-ounce) loaf fat-free pound cake
2 cups raspberries
¼ cup fat-free frozen whipped topping, thawed

exchanges:
2 Starch
1 Fruit

1. Slice pound cake into 4 slices; cut each slice into 2 triangles, and place evenly on each of 4 plates. Top each serving with ½ cup raspberries and 1 tablespoon whipped topping. Yield: 4 servings.

per serving: Calories 198; Carbohydrate 43.2g; Fat 1.0g (saturated 0.2g); Fiber 4.8g; Protein 3.6g; Cholesterol 0mg; Sodium 196mg; Calcium 38mg; Iron 1.5mg

Raspberry Trifle

This colorful combination makes a stunning addition to your buffet.

POINTS:
3

½ (16-ounce) loaf fat-free pound cake
3 (3.5-ounce) cartons vanilla fat-free pudding
1½ cups raspberries

exchanges:
1 Starch
1 Fruit

1. Cut pound cake into cubes; place cubes on bottom of a 2-quart glass bowl or trifle dish. Top with pudding and raspberries. Yield: 6 servings.

per serving: Calories 152; Carbohydrate 31.2g; Fat 0.2g (saturated 0.0g); Fiber 2.6g; Protein 2.6g; Cholesterol 0mg; Sodium 202mg; Calcium 61mg; Iron 1.0mg

---

⁂

Enjoy Brownies Anytime!

If you love fudgy brownies, but you're tempted to eat the whole pan, read on! Below and on the following page, you'll find three delicious desserts that use only *part* of a pan of brownies. The remaining brownies go in the freezer for "safekeeping."

To get started, pick a mix, and follow the directions on the box to make a 13 x 9-inch pan of brownies. Once they've cooled, cut the brownies into 18 (2-inch) squares. Set aside the brownies needed for the recipe you're preparing. Then, wrap each remaining brownie individually in plastic wrap, place inside a freezer-proof zip-top bag, and freeze. The next time you crave a brownie or need a quick dessert, simply choose the number of brownies you need, and let them thaw at room temperature.

Here's a quick breakdown of **POINTS** values for popular low-fat brownie mixes. We used a 20.5-ounce box of Betty Crocker Sweet Rewards Fudge Brownie mix in our recipes. The **POINTS** and nutritional analyses reflect that.

Betty Crocker Sweet Rewards Fudge Brownie mix	3 **POINTS**
Krusteaz Fudge Brownie mix	2 **POINTS**
Pillsbury Fudge Brownie mix *(prepared according to low-fat directions)*	3 **POINTS**

POINTS values reflect ¹/₁₈th of each prepared mix.

---

total time ⁂ 7 minutes

Brownie Sundae for One

1 (2-inch-square) low-fat brownie (such as Betty Crocker Sweet Rewards)

⅓ cup vanilla fat-free ice cream

1 tablespoon raspberry fruit spread, melted

POINTS:

5

exchanges:

3½ Starch

1. Place brownie on a dessert plate. Top with ice cream, and drizzle with raspberry spread. Yield: 1 sundae.

per serving: Calories 238; Carbohydrate 52.6g; Fat 2.5g (saturated 1.0g); Fiber 1.0g; Protein 4.0g; Cholesterol 0mg; Sodium 146mg; Calcium 53mg; Iron 1.1mg

Upside-Down Brownie Splits

POINTS:

5

exchanges:

4 Starch

1⅓ cups vanilla fat-free no-sugar-added ice cream

1   large banana, peeled and sliced

4   (2-inch-square) low-fat brownies (such as Betty Crocker Sweet
     Rewards)

¼   cup fat-free chocolate syrup

1. Scoop ⅓ cup ice cream into each of 4 dessert dishes; top evenly with banana. Microwave brownies at HIGH 20 seconds or until warm. Crumble brownies evenly over banana. Top each serving with 1 tablespoon chocolate syrup. Yield: 4 servings.

per serving: Calories 267; Carbohydrate 58.6g; Fat 2.9g (saturated 1.2g); Fiber 2.3g; Protein 5.5g; Cholesterol 0mg; Sodium 170mg; Calcium 76mg; Iron 1.8mg

Individual Brownie Cakes

POINTS:

5

exchanges:

3 Starch

½ Fat

4   (2-inch-square) low-fat brownies (such as Betty Crocker Sweet
     Rewards)

8   teaspoons raspberry fruit spread

⅓   cup chocolate fudge reduced-fat frosting

1. Cut each brownie in half lengthwise. Spread 2 teaspoons fruit spread on bottom half of each brownie, and top each with remaining brownie half. Melt frosting in microwave at HIGH 45 seconds or until thin and smooth. Pour frosting evenly over brownies, spreading on tops and sides of brownies. Yield: 4 servings.

per serving: Calories 238; Carbohydrate 48.6g; Fat 4.5g (saturated 1.7g); Fiber 1.0g; Protein 2.0g; Cholesterol 0mg; Sodium 160mg; Calcium 0mg; Iron 1.6mg

fish
&
shellfish

Country Catfish photo, facing page

What a surprise! The delicious crispy fish is oven-fried.

POINTS:

5

exchanges:

1 Starch

4 Lean Meat

per serving:

Calories 250

Carbohydrate 18.7g

Fat 5.0g (saturated 1.3g)

Fiber 0.6g

Protein 31.5g

Cholesterol 99mg

Sodium 410mg

Calcium 30mg

Iron 4.3mg

Butter-flavored cooking spray

⅔   cup corn flake crumbs

¼   teaspoon salt

¼   teaspoon ground red pepper

4   (6-ounce) farm-raised catfish fillets

2   egg whites, lightly beaten

½   cup commercial corn relish

1. Preheat oven to 450°.

2. Line a shallow pan with aluminum foil. Coat with cooking spray.

3. Combine crumbs, salt, and pepper in a small bowl; stir well. Dip fish in beaten egg whites; dredge in crumb mixture. Place fish in pan. Bake at 450° for 8 to 10 minutes or until fish flakes easily when tested with a fork. Serve immediately with corn relish. Yield: 4 servings (serving size: 1 fillet and 2 tablespoons relish).

Serve with: sliced tomatoes

Zesty Coleslaw (page 133)

cold watermelon wedges

Country Catfish,
recipe, facing page

Zesty Coleslaw,
recipe, page 133

**Linguine and
Mussels Marinara**
recipe, page 56

Sweet-and-Sour Shrimp
recipe, page 58

Baked Won Ton Crisps
recipe, page 18

Grilled Honey-Balsamic Salmon
recipe, facing page

Lemon-Asparagus Packets
recipe, page 178

Grilled Honey-Balsamic Salmon photo, facing page

**A tangy glaze brushed over the salmon just before grilling
creates a delectable main dish in minutes.**

1½ tablespoons honey
1½ tablespoons Dijon mustard
1 tablespoon balsamic vinegar
¼ teaspoon coarsely ground pepper
¼ teaspoon garlic salt
2 (6-ounce) salmon steaks (½ inch thick)
Cooking spray

1. Prepare grill.

2. Combine first 5 ingredients in a bowl; brush mixture over fish.

3. Place fish on grill rack coated with cooking spray; cover and grill 2 to 3 minutes on each side or until fish flakes easily when tested with a fork. Serve immediately. Yield: 2 servings.

Serve with: hot cooked orzo or other small pasta
Lemon-Asparagus Packets (page 178)

POINTS:

6

exchanges:

1 Starch
4½ Lean Meat

per serving:

Calories 266
Carbohydrate 15.8g
Fat 7.0g (saturated 1.0g)
Fiber 0.2g
Protein 34.8g
Cholesterol 88mg
Sodium 627mg
Calcium 43mg
Iron 1.8mg

Broiled Flounder with Pineapple Salsa

Radishes and red pepper add a refreshing bite to the sweet fruit topping.

POINTS:

3

exchanges:

½ Fruit

4 Very Lean Meat

per serving:

Calories 165

Carbohydrate 6.6g

Fat 1.9g (saturated 0.4g)

Fiber 0.7g

Protein 28.4g

Cholesterol 80mg

Sodium 275mg

Calcium 24mg

Iron 0.6mg

4   (6-ounce) flounder fillets

Butter-flavored spray (such as I Can't Believe It's Not Butter)

2   teaspoons salt-free lemon-herb seasoning

¼   teaspoon salt

1   (8-ounce) can crushed pineapple in juice, drained

3   green onions, sliced

⅓   cup chopped radishes

½   teaspoon dried crushed red pepper

1. Preheat broiler.

2. Place fish on a broiler pan coated with butter spray. Coat fish with butter spray; sprinkle with lemon-herb seasoning and salt.

3. Broil 8 minutes or until fish flakes easily when tested with a fork.

4. While fish broils, combine pineapple and remaining ingredients. Top each fillet with ¼ cup pineapple salsa. Serve immediately. Yield: 4 servings.

Serve with: steamed sugar snap peas
warm dinner rolls

---

total time ✳ 9 minutes

Grouper Athenian photo, page 1

**This striking yet simple Greek entrée will win you applause.
Substitute plain feta cheese for the flavored, if desired.**

4   (6-ounce) grouper fillets
2   teaspoons salt-free Greek seasoning
Cooking spray
1   (10-ounce) package frozen chopped spinach, thawed and squeezed dry
1   plum tomato, coarsely chopped
¼   cup (1 ounce) crumbled basil- and tomato-flavored feta cheese

1. Sprinkle both sides of fish with seasoning. Coat a large nonstick skillet with cooking spray, and place over medium-high heat until hot. Add fish, and cook 3 minutes; remove skillet from heat.

2. Turn fish; top with spinach, tomato, and cheese. Return skillet to heat; cover and cook 3 to 4 minutes or until spinach is hot and fish flakes easily when tested with a fork. Serve immediately. Yield: 4 servings.

> **Serve with:** hot cooked angel hair pasta
> Honeybee Sundaes (page 27)

POINTS:

4

exchanges:

5 Very Lean Meat

per serving:

Calories 197
Carbohydrate 3.6g
Fat 3.8g (saturated 1.6g)
Fiber 2.3g
Protein 36.4g
Cholesterol 68mg
Sodium 230mg
Calcium 146mg
Iron 3.0mg

Citrus-Jerk Orange Roughy

Jerk is a spicy Jamaican seasoning blend that can also be used as a dry rub on beef, pork, chicken, and lamb.

POINTS:
4

exchanges:
1 Starch
3 Very Lean Meat

per serving:
Calories 179
Carbohydrate 14.0g
Fat 2.3g (saturated 0.2g)
Fiber 0.0g
Protein 25.1g
Cholesterol 34mg
Sodium 418mg
Calcium 59mg
Iron 0.4mg

4   (6-ounce) orange roughy fillets
1   tablespoon plus 1 teaspoon jerk seasoning
Cooking spray
1   teaspoon olive oil
4   tablespoons orange marmalade
3   tablespoons water
2   tablespoons lemon juice
1/8 teaspoon cracked pepper

1. Sprinkle both sides of fish evenly with seasoning, pressing gently to adhere. Coat a large nonstick skillet with cooking spray; add oil, and place over medium-high heat until hot. Add fish; cook 3 minutes on each side or until fish flakes easily when tested with a fork. Remove from skillet; set aside, and keep warm.

2. Add orange marmalade and remaining ingredients to skillet. Bring to a boil, and cook 1 minute. Pour sauce over fish, and serve immediately. Yield: 4 servings.

Serve with: Black Bean-Rice Salad (page 139)
fresh cubed pineapple

Sunflower Orange Roughy

Heart-healthy sunflower seeds make this crust extra-crisp and crunchy.

¼   cup corn flake crumbs
2   tablespoons dry-roasted sunflower kernels
1   teaspoon salt-free seasoning
4   (6-ounce) orange roughy fillets
1   tablespoon lemon juice
Cooking spray

1. Preheat oven to 425°.

2. Combine first 3 ingredients in a small bowl. Dip fish in lemon juice, and dredge in crumb mixture.

3. Place fish on rack of a broiler pan coated with cooking spray. Sprinkle any remaining crumb mixture over fish. Bake at 425° for 10 minutes or until fish flakes easily when tested with a fork. Serve immediately. Yield: 4 servings.

POINTS:
3

exchanges:
½ Starch
4 Very Lean Meat

per serving:
Calories 162
Carbohydrate 5.8g
Fat 3.2g (saturated 0.2g)
Fiber 0.5g
Protein 26.3g
Cholesterol 34mg
Sodium 167mg
Calcium 54mg
Iron 1.8mg

Serve with: steamed frozen mixed vegetables
Garlic-Dill Rolls (page 14)

Orange-Glazed Salmon

This succulent Asian-style salmon cooks in just one pan.

POINTS:
5

exchanges:
5 Lean Meat

per serving:
Calories 216
Carbohydrate 2.1g
Fat 6.5g (saturated 1.0g)
Fiber 0.1g
Protein 34.8g
Cholesterol 88mg
Sodium 713mg
Calcium 24mg
Iron 1.3mg

4   (6-ounce) salmon fillets (1 inch thick)
¼   teaspoon salt
¼   teaspoon pepper
Cooking spray
3   tablespoons low-sodium soy sauce
3   tablespoons orange juice
½   teaspoon dark sesame oil

1. Sprinkle fish with salt and pepper. Coat a large nonstick skillet with cooking spray; place over high heat until hot. Add fish, and cook, uncovered, 3 minutes on each side. Cover and cook 3 minutes or until fish flakes easily when tested with a fork. Remove from skillet; set aside, and keep warm.

2. Add soy sauce and orange juice to skillet; cook over high heat 1 minute, stirring to deglaze skillet. Add oil, and stir well. Pour sauce over fish, and serve immediately. Yield: 4 servings.

Serve with: hot cooked rice
Buttery Snow Peas (page 181)

Red Snapper Vera Cruz

You control the spiciness of this rich tomato sauce!
Use mild, medium, or hot salsa depending on the heat your taste buds can handle.

Garlic-flavored or regular cooking spray

4   (6-ounce) red snapper or orange roughy fillets

½   teaspoon ground cumin

1   (8-ounce) can Mexican-style or regular stewed tomatoes, undrained

⅓   cup salsa

¼   cup chopped fresh cilantro or parsley

1. Coat a large nonstick skillet with cooking spray; place over medium-high heat until hot. Sprinkle one side of fillets with cumin.

2. Place fish, seasoned side down, in skillet; cook 3 minutes. Turn fish; top with tomatoes and salsa. Reduce heat, and simmer, uncovered, 5 minutes or until fish flakes easily when tested with a fork. Sprinkle with cilantro. Serve immediately. Yield: 4 servings.

Serve with: hot cooked yellow saffron rice
                  warm French rolls

POINTS:

4

exchanges:

1 Vegetable

5 Very Lean Meat

per serving:

Calories 193

Carbohydrate 5.5g

Fat 2.4g (saturated 0.5g)

Fiber 1.3g

Protein 35.7g

Cholesterol 63mg

Sodium 383mg

Calcium 73mg

Iron 0.8mg

Cajun-Style Swordfish

Serve this fish between slices of crusty French bread as a sandwich.

POINTS:
5

exchanges:
5 Very Lean Meat

per serving:
Calories 226
Carbohydrate 4.1g
Fat 7.4g (saturated 2.0g)
Fiber 0.5g
Protein 33.7g
Cholesterol 68mg
Sodium 487mg
Calcium 8.3mg
Iron 1.4mg

4   (6-ounce) swordfish fillets (1 inch thick)
Olive oil-flavored cooking spray
1½ teaspoons blackening seasoning, divided
⅓   cup fat-free mayonnaise
1   tablespoon sweet pickle relish
1   teaspoon fresh lemon juice
Lemon wedges (optional)

1. Preheat broiler.

2. Coat both sides of fish with cooking spray; sprinkle evenly with 1¼ teaspoons blackening seasoning. Place fish on broiler pan coated with cooking spray. Broil 6 minutes on each side or until fish flakes easily when tested with a fork.

3. While fish broils, combine mayonnaise, remaining ¼ teaspoon seasoning, relish, and lemon juice, stirring well. Serve fish immediately with mayonnaise mixture and, if desired, lemon wedges. Yield: 4 servings.

Serve with: Skillet Zucchini (page 185)
crusty French bread

---

total time ❊ 12 minutes

Tuna Pasta Primavera

**What better way to celebrate spring than with a colorful pasta dish
that combines fresh asparagus and tomatoes.**

8	ounces bow tie pasta, uncooked
1	pound fresh asparagus
1	cup frozen English peas
¼	cup sliced green onions
½	teaspoon salt
2	teaspoons olive oil
1	cup chopped seeded tomato
¼	cup lemon juice
2	(6-ounce) cans low-sodium white tuna packed in water, drained and coarsely flaked
½	teaspoon freshly ground pepper

1. Cook pasta according to package directions, omitting salt and fat; drain, reserving 3 tablespoons of pasta water.

2. While pasta cooks, snap off tough ends of asparagus. Cut asparagus into 1-inch pieces.

3. Combine asparagus and peas in a steamer basket over boiling water. Cover and steam 3 to 4 minutes or until asparagus is crisp-tender. Drain.

4. Combine steamed vegetables, green onions, salt, and olive oil in a large bowl. Add pasta, reserved pasta water, tomato, and lemon juice; toss well. Add tuna; toss. Sprinkle with freshly ground pepper. Yield: 6 servings.

POINTS:

5

exchanges:

2 Starch
1 Vegetable
1 Lean Meat

per serving:
Calories 249
Carbohydrate 36.0g
Fat 3.8g (saturated 0.7g)
Fiber 3.5g
Protein 18.3g
Cholesterol 18mg
Sodium 387mg
Calcium 36mg
Iron 2.8mg

Serve with: warm whole wheat rolls
Strawberries and Cream (page 25)

Tuna Steaks with Salsa

Made with fresh vegetables and lots of ripe tomatoes, salsa is a nutritious super-food packed full of Vitamin C and cancer-fighting antioxidants.

POINTS:
6

exchanges:
1 Vegetable
5 Lean Meat

per serving:
Calories 263
Carbohydrate 3.4g
Fat 8.5g (saturated 2.1g)
Fiber 0.6g
Protein 40.3g
Cholesterol 64mg
Sodium 430mg
Calcium 26mg
Iron 1.8mg

4   (6-ounce) tuna steaks (½ inch thick)
     Olive oil-flavored cooking spray
½   teaspoon salt-free garlic-herb seasoning
1   cup chunky salsa

1. Lightly coat both sides of fish with cooking spray; sprinkle both sides with seasoning. Coat a large nonstick skillet with cooking spray. Place over medium-high heat until hot. Add fish; cook 2 minutes on each side or to desired degree of doneness. Serve immediately with salsa. Yield: 4 servings.

Serve with: Zucchini Sticks (page 185)
crusty sourdough rolls

Angel Hair Pasta with Clams

You may be surprised to learn that these small shellfish are rich in iron.
They're delicious cooked with simple seasonings and served over a hot bed of pasta.

8   ounces angel hair pasta, uncooked
1   teaspoon olive oil
1½ teaspoons minced garlic
3   (6½-ounce) cans minced clams
2   tablespoons shredded fresh Parmesan cheese
Freshly ground pepper

POINTS:
6

exchanges:
3 Starch
1 Lean Meat

1. Cook pasta according to package directions, omitting salt and fat.

2. While pasta cooks, heat oil in a large nonstick skillet over medium heat. Add garlic; sauté 2 minutes. Drain clams, reserving liquid. Add clam liquid to skillet, and simmer 5 minutes. Add clams; simmer 5 minutes.

3. Combine drained pasta and clam mixture in a serving bowl; toss gently. Sprinkle with cheese and pepper. Serve immediately. Yield: 4 servings.

per serving:
Calories 310
Carbohydrate 47.0g
Fat 3.8g (saturated 1.1g)
Fiber 1.4g
Protein 19.6g
Cholesterol 47mg
Sodium 849mg
Calcium 56mg
Iron 3.9mg

Serve with: steamed fresh or frozen broccoli spears

Linguine and Mussels Marinara photo, page 42

**You'll want to serve this saucy mussel dish in bowls with a piece
of crusty bread so you can sop up every last drop of sauce.**

POINTS:
6

exchanges:
4 Starch
1 Lean Meat

per serving:
Calories 342
Carbohydrate 57.9g
Fat 4.4g (saturated 0.4g)
Fiber 9.8g
Protein 16.4g
Cholesterol 16mg
Sodium 654mg
Calcium 50mg
Iron 4.9mg

8   ounces linguine, uncooked
1   pound fresh, farm-raised mussels
2   cups low-fat chunky pasta sauce
¼   teaspoon crushed red pepper flakes
¼   cup chopped fresh basil

1. Cook pasta according to package directions, omitting salt and fat.

2. While pasta cooks, rinse mussels in cold water; remove beards on mussels, and scrub shells with a brush. Discard opened or cracked mussels. Combine mussels, pasta sauce, and red pepper flakes in a large deep skillet. Cover and bring to a simmer over medium heat; cook 5 minutes or until mussels open. (Discard any unopened mussels.)

3. Place ¾ cup drained pasta into each of 4 bowls. Top evenly with mussels and sauce; sprinkle with basil. Serve immediately. Yield: 4 servings.

Serve with: mixed salad greens
low-fat vinaigrette
Garlic Bread (page 12)

Grilled Scallops and Tomatoes

Stop by a farmer's market to get the freshest tomatoes and corn.

1½ pounds fresh sea scallops
20 cherry tomatoes
¼ cup low-sodium teriyaki sauce
Cooking spray

1. Prepare grill.

2. Place scallops and tomatoes alternately on 4 (12-inch) skewers; brush with 2 tablespoons teriyaki sauce.

3. Place kabobs on grill rack coated with cooking spray, and grill, uncovered, 5 minutes. Turn kabobs, and brush with remaining teriyaki sauce; grill 10 minutes or until scallops are opaque. Serve immediately. Yield: 4 servings.

> **Serve with:** Dilled Corn on the Cob (page 181)
> Spinach-Onion Salad (page 137)

POINTS:
4

exchanges:
2 Vegetable
4 Very Lean Meat

per serving:
Calories 183
Carbohydrate 11.0g
Fat 1.6g (saturated 0.2g)
Fiber 0.9g
Protein 30.3g
Cholesterol 56mg
Sodium 602mg
Calcium 45mg
Iron 0.9mg

Sweet-and-Sour Shrimp photo, page 43

To capture the extra sauce be sure to serve this stir-fry over rice.

POINTS:
3

exchanges:
1 Starch
2 Lean Meat

per serving:
Calories 139
Carbohydrate 13.8g
Fat 3.1g (saturated 0.5g)
Fiber 1.5g
Protein 14.1g
Cholesterol 121mg
Sodium 652mg
Calcium 40mg
Iron 2.4mg

1 (8-ounce) can pineapple chunks in juice
1 teaspoon cornstarch
3 tablespoons chili sauce
1 tablespoon low-sodium soy sauce
½ teaspoon garlic powder
Cooking spray
2 teaspoons sesame or vegetable oil
1 green bell pepper, coarsely chopped
½ onion, sliced
¾ pound peeled and deveined fresh shrimp

1. Drain pineapple, reserving juice; set pineapple chunks aside. Combine reserved juice, cornstarch, and next 3 ingredients; set aside.

2. Coat a large nonstick skillet or wok with cooking spray, and add oil. Place over medium-high heat until hot. Add green pepper and onion; stir-fry 2 to 3 minutes or until crisp-tender. Add shrimp; stir-fry 2 to 3 minutes or until shrimp turn pink.

3. Stir cornstarch mixture and pineapple chunks into shrimp mixture. Cook over medium heat, stirring constantly, until mixture is thickened and bubbly. Serve immediately. Yield: 4 servings.

> **Serve with:** hot cooked rice
> Baked Won Ton Crisps (page 18)

Polenta with Shrimp and Tomato Sauce

A staple in Italy, polenta is a soft corn mixture that can be served in place of pasta. Look for refrigerated polenta in the produce section of the grocery.

Olive oil-flavored cooking spray
1   (16-ounce) package refrigerated polenta, cut into 12 slices
¾   pound peeled and deveined fresh shrimp
2   cups low-fat chunky pasta sauce
3   tablespoons shredded fresh Parmesan cheese

1. Coat a large nonstick skillet with cooking spray; place over medium-high heat until hot.

2. Arrange polenta slices in skillet; cook 4 minutes on each side or until edges are crisp. Remove from skillet, and keep warm.

3. Coat skillet with cooking spray. Add shrimp, and cook 2 to 3 minutes or until shrimp turn pink. Stir in pasta sauce; cook 2 to 3 minutes or until thoroughly heated.

4. Place 3 slices of polenta on each of 4 serving plates. Spoon shrimp and sauce evenly over polenta; sprinkle with Parmesan cheese. Serve immediately. Yield: 4 servings.

POINTS:
4

exchanges:
2 Starch
2½ Very Lean Meat

per serving:
Calories 238
Carbohydrate 26.0g
Fat 3.0g (saturated 1.2g)
Fiber 4.0g
Protein 23.2g
Cholesterol 133mg
Sodium 799mg
Calcium 109mg
Iron 3.4mg

Serve with: mixed salad greens
low-fat olive-oil vinaigrette

Zesty Fettuccine and Shrimp

The secret to this timesaving recipe is buying the shrimp already peeled and deveined. You'll find it in the fresh seafood department of the grocery store.

POINTS:
7

exchanges:
3 Starch
2 Lean Meat

per serving:
Calories 344
Carbohydrate 48.2g
Fat 4.9g (saturated 0.7g)
Fiber 1.7g
Protein 25.2g
Cholesterol 129mg
Sodium 492mg
Calcium 71mg
Iron 4.6mg

8   ounces fettuccine, uncooked
    Olive oil-flavored cooking spray
2   teaspoons olive oil
2   teaspoons blackening seasoning
¾   pound peeled and deveined large fresh shrimp
2   tablespoons lemon juice
1   (14½-ounce) can diced tomatoes with roasted garlic, drained
¼   teaspoon pepper

1. Cook pasta according to package directions, omitting salt and fat.

2. While pasta cooks, coat a large nonstick skillet with cooking spray, and add oil. Place over medium-high heat until hot. Sprinkle blackening seasoning evenly over shrimp. Add shrimp to skillet; cook 2 minutes on each side or until shrimp turn pink. Stir in lemon juice. Add tomatoes and pepper; cook until thoroughly heated.

3. Spoon shrimp mixture over drained pasta, and serve immediately. Yield: 4 servings.

Serve with: mixed salad greens low-fat vinaigrette crusty sourdough bread

**Fresh Tomato Pizza
with Gorgonzola Cheese**
recipe, page 77

Cheesy Bean Casserole
recipe, page 67

Skillet Corn Bread
recipe, page 15

**Mediterranean Pasta
with Zucchini**
recipe, page 73

Fettuccine with Blue Cheese-Artichoke Sauce
recipe, page 72

meatless
main
dishes

Speedy Quesadillas photo, page 173

Quesadillas overflowing with cheese beat the plain turkey sandwich any day.

POINTS:

4

exchanges:

1½ Starch

1 Medium-Fat Meat

per serving:

Calories 198

Carbohydrate 25.0g

Fat 5.6g (saturated 3.2g)

Fiber 1.2g

Protein 11.6g

Cholesterol 18mg

Sodium 550mg

Calcium 200mg

Iron 1.0mg

Butter-flavored cooking spray

4   (8-inch) fat-free flour tortillas

1   cup (4 ounces) preshredded reduced-fat Cheddar cheese

¼   cup chopped green onions

1. Coat a large nonstick skillet with cooking spray; place over medium-high heat. Place 1 tortilla in skillet, and top with ½ cup cheese, 2 tablespoons onions, and another tortilla. Cook 2 minutes on each side or until lightly browned. Remove from skillet, and keep warm. Repeat with remaining tortillas, cheese, and onions. Cut each quesadilla into 6 wedges. Yield: 4 servings (serving size: 3 wedges).

> **Serve with:** salsa and fat-free sour cream
> Sausage and Black Bean Soup (page 172)
> chilled grapes

Cheesy Bean Casserole photo, page 62

The beans and cheese pack this casserole full of good-for-you fiber and calcium.

Cooking spray

1   cup chopped onion

2   (15-ounce) cans chile-hot kidney beans, drained

2   (14½-ounce) cans no-salt-added whole tomatoes, drained and
      chopped

½   teaspoon garlic powder

¼   teaspoon pepper

1   cup (4 ounces) preshredded reduced-fat sharp Cheddar cheese

1. Preheat oven to 400°.

2. Coat a nonstick skillet with cooking spray; place over medium-high heat until hot. Add onion; sauté until tender. Stir in beans and next 3 ingredients. Cook 3 minutes or until thoroughly heated, stirring well.

3. Spoon mixture into 4 individual baking dishes or 1 (8-inch) square baking dish; sprinkle with cheese. Bake, uncovered, at 400° for 5 minutes or until cheese melts. Let stand 5 minutes. Yield: 4 servings.

POINTS:

5

exchanges:

2 Starch

1 Vegetable

1 Medium-Fat Meat

per serving:

Calories 274

Carbohydrate 35.4g

Fat 6.9g (saturated 4.1g)

Fiber 12.8g

Protein 17.6g

Cholesterol 20mg

Sodium 257mg

Calcium 250mg

Iron 0.8mg

Serve with: Skillet Corn Bread (page 15)

Southwestern Vegetable Bake

Need a meal that practically makes itself? Try this combine-and-bake casserole.

POINTS:

5

exchanges:

3 Starch

2 Vegetable

1 Fat

per serving:

Calories 267

Carbohydrate 49.3g

Fat 6.0g (saturated 3.2g)

Fiber 9.2g

Protein 10.9g

Cholesterol 15mg

Sodium 1290mg

Calcium 152mg

Iron 2.7mg

2 (11-ounce) cans whole-kernel corn with sweet peppers, drained

1 (14½-ounce) can chili-style tomatoes, undrained

1 (15½-ounce) can white hominy, drained

1 (15-ounce) can no-salt-added black beans, rinsed and drained

¼ teaspoon pepper

½ cup (2 ounces) shredded Monterey Jack cheese with jalapeño peppers

1. Preheat oven to 350°.

2. Combine first 5 ingredients in a 2-quart baking dish; stir well. Cover and bake at 350° for 25 minutes or until bubbly. Uncover, sprinkle with cheese, and bake 5 minutes. Yield: 4 servings.

Serve with: fresh strawberry slices
fat-free or 1% low-fat milk

Black Bean Burritos

Leftover burritos make a quick lunch-on-the-go the next day.

1   (12-ounce) jar fat-free black bean dip
4   (10-inch) fat-free flour tortillas
1   cup chopped tomato
¾   cup chopped onion
1   cup chopped green bell pepper
Salsa (optional)
Fat-free sour cream (optional)

1. Spread dip evenly over tortillas (about ⅓ cup dip per tortilla). Sprinkle evenly with tomato, onion, and green pepper.

2. To serve, roll up tortillas. If desired, top with salsa and sour cream. Yield: 4 servings.

> **Serve with:** Marinated Tomatoes (page 139)
> juicy tangerines

POINTS:

4

exchanges:

2 Starch
2 Vegetable

per serving:

Calories 225
Carbohydrate 44.4g
Fat 0.3g (saturated 0.0g)
Fiber 5.4g
Protein 9.9g
Cholesterol 0mg
Sodium 645mg
Calcium 12mg
Iron 2.5mg

Vegetarian Tacos

Perfect for the nights when the family can't eat together. Simply make the filling ahead, and let each person top their own tacos as they come in the door.

POINTS:

7

exchanges:

2 Starch

1 Vegetable

2 Medium-Fat Meat

per serving:

Calories 334

Carbohydrate 34.4g

Fat 12.5g (saturated 3.8g)

Fiber 6.1g

Protein 20.3g

Cholesterol 17mg

Sodium 494mg

Calcium 378mg

Iron 4.4mg

1½ cups frozen burger-style vegetable protein crumbles, thawed
1   (8-ounce) can no-salt-added tomato sauce
1   small onion, chopped
1   teaspoon minced garlic
2   teaspoons chili powder
1   teaspoon ground cumin
8   taco shells

Taco Bar Toppings
1   small onion, chopped
1   green bell pepper, chopped
½   head lettuce, shredded
½   (10-ounce) package shredded carrots
1   (15-ounce) can no-salt-added black beans, rinsed and drained
½   cup (2 ounces) preshredded reduced-fat Cheddar cheese
½   cup (2 ounces) preshredded part-skim mozzarella cheese

1. Combine first 6 ingredients in a saucepan. Bring to a boil; cover, reduce heat, and simmer 10 minutes or until mixture is thoroughly heated. While protein crumble mixture cooks, prepare Taco Bar Toppings.

2. Spoon mixture evenly into taco shells. Top with equal amounts of Taco Bar Toppings. Yield: 4 servings (serving size: 2 tacos).

Serve with: fresh raspberries
fat-free or 1% low-fat milk

Confetti Cheese Omelet

Great for breakfast but hearty enough for dinner, omelets are a fun option any night of the week.

Cooking spray

¼ cup chopped red bell pepper

¼ cup chopped green or orange bell pepper

¼ cup sliced green onions

1 cup egg substitute

¼ teaspoon salt

¼ teaspoon freshly ground pepper

½ cup (2 ounces) preshredded reduced-fat sharp Cheddar cheese

1. Coat a 10-inch nonstick skillet with cooking spray; place over medium heat until hot. Add peppers and onions; cook 4 minutes, stirring occasionally.

2. Pour egg substitute into skillet; sprinkle with salt and pepper. Cook, without stirring, 2 to 3 minutes or until golden brown on bottom. Sprinkle with cheese. Loosen omelet with a spatula; fold in half. Cook 2 minutes or until egg mixture is set and cheese begins to melt.

3. Cut omelet in half. Slide halves onto serving plates. Yield: 2 servings.

POINTS:

4

exchanges:

1 Vegetable

3 Lean Meat

per serving:

Calories 159

Carbohydrate 5.3g

Fat 5.9g (saturated 3.2g)

Fiber 0.7g

Protein 20.7g

Cholesterol 19mg

Sodium 680mg

Calcium 247mg

Iron 2.4mg

> **Serve with:** toasted English muffins
> fresh strawberries
> hot coffee

Fettuccine with Blue Cheese-Artichoke Sauce <small>photo, page 64</small>

Upgrade traditional fettuccine and alfredo sauce with artichokes and blue cheese.

POINTS:
6

exchanges:
3 Starch
1 High-Fat Meat

per serving:
Calories 313
Carbohydrate 45.7g
Fat 8.5g (saturated 4.1g)
Fiber 2.6g
Protein 14.7g
Cholesterol 25mg
Sodium 691mg
Calcium 137mg
Iron 2.7mg

1 (9-ounce) package refrigerated fettuccine
   Cooking spray
1 (14-ounce) can quartered artichoke hearts, drained
1 cup sliced fresh mushrooms
1 (10-ounce) container refrigerated light alfredo sauce
2 tablespoons crumbled blue cheese

1. Cook pasta according to package directions, omitting salt and fat.

2. While pasta cooks, coat a large nonstick skillet with cooking spray; place over medium-high heat until hot. Add artichokes and mushrooms; cook 3 to 4 minutes or until mushrooms are tender. Add alfredo sauce to artichoke mixture; cook until thoroughly heated.

3. Place drained pasta in a large bowl. Pour sauce mixture over pasta; toss to combine. Sprinkle with cheese. Yield: 4 (1¼-cup) servings.

> **Serve with:** Tossed Apple Salad (page 130) or sliced apples
> warm soft breadsticks

Mediterranean Pasta with Zucchini photo, page 63

This one-skillet supper bursts with the flavors of Italy.

8	ounces penne or ziti pasta, uncooked
1	(14½-ounce) can diced tomatoes with basil, garlic, and oregano
1	(15-ounce) can chickpeas (garbanzo beans), drained
1	zucchini, sliced
2	tablespoons sliced ripe olives

1. Cook pasta according to package directions, omitting salt and fat.

2. While pasta cooks, combine tomatoes and remaining 3 ingredients in a large skillet; bring to a boil. Reduce heat, and simmer, uncovered, 5 minutes. Spoon tomato mixture over drained pasta. Yield: 4 (2-cup) servings.

> **Serve with:** warm pita bread
> fresh pear slices

POINTS:

7

exchanges:

4 Starch

1 Vegetable

½ Fat

per serving:

Calories 363

Carbohydrate 67.5g

Fat 3.6g (saturated 0.3g)

Fiber 3.2g

Protein 14.4g

Cholesterol 0mg

Sodium 458mg

Calcium 95mg

Iron 4.1mg

Tortellini Primavera with Pesto Sauce

Using prepared pesto makes this pasta and sauce a snap to prepare.

POINTS:

7

exchanges:

2 Starch

2 Vegetable

1 High-Fat Meat

1 Fat

per serving:

Calories 331

Carbohydrate 38.1g

Fat 12.2g (saturated 4.5g)

Fiber 3.0g

Protein 18.7g

Cholesterol 32mg

Sodium 659mg

Calcium 409mg

Iron 1.5mg

1	(9-ounce) package refrigerated cheese tortellini
1	(16-ounce) package frozen broccoli stir-fry vegetables
1	(8-ounce) carton fat-free sour cream
2	tablespoons commercial pesto
¼	teaspoon salt
¼	cup (1 ounce) grated fresh Parmesan cheese
⅛	teaspoon freshly ground pepper

1. Cook tortellini and vegetables in 3 quarts boiling water 5 to 7 minutes or until vegetables and pasta are tender. Drain and return to pan.

2. Combine sour cream, pesto, and salt, stirring well. Gently stir sour cream mixture into pasta mixture. Sprinkle with Parmesan cheese and pepper. Serve immediately. Yield: 4 (1¼-cup) servings.

Serve with: Balsamic Tomato Salad (page 138)
warm soft breadsticks

Skillet Ziti and Vegetables photo, page 2

**An herbed pasta sauce will add extra flavors and seasonings
that a regular pasta sauce just can't give you.**

2	cups low-fat roasted garlic or herb pasta sauce
2	cups water
8	ounces ziti pasta, uncooked
1	(10-ounce) package fresh stir-fry vegetables (about 2½ cups)
¾	cup (3 ounces) shredded provolone cheese

1. Combine pasta sauce and water in a large skillet; bring to a boil. Add pasta and vegetables. Cover, reduce heat, and simmer 15 minutes or until pasta is tender.

2. Remove from heat, and sprinkle with cheese. Yield: 6 (1¼-cup) servings.

Serve with: crusty rolls
chocolate fat-free ice cream

POINTS:

4

exchanges:

2 Starch
2 Vegetable
1 Fat

per serving:

Calories 244
Carbohydrate 39.6g
Fat 4.9g (saturated 2.5g)
Fiber 4.1g
Protein 11.2g
Cholesterol 10mg
Sodium 395mg
Calcium 134mg
Iron 1.8mg

Mushroom Pizza

Your kids will love these hand-sized pizza squares.

POINTS:

7

exchanges:

2 Starch

2 Vegetable

1 High-Fat Meat

per serving:

Calories 315

Carbohydrate 40.2g

Fat 9.4g (saturated 3.6g)

Fiber 2.6g

Protein 16.6g

Cholesterol 21mg

Sodium 833mg

Calcium 302mg

Iron 2.4mg

1   (10-ounce) can refrigerated pizza crust dough

Cooking spray

1   teaspoon dried Italian seasoning

½   cup pizza sauce

1   (8-ounce) package sliced mushrooms

1¼ cups (5 ounces) preshredded part-skim mozzarella cheese

1. Preheat oven to 425°.

2. Unroll pizza crust dough, and place on a baking sheet coated with cooking spray; press to a 14- x 10-inch rectangle. Sprinkle dough with Italian seasoning. Bake at 425° for 7 minutes.

3. Spread pizza sauce over crust; top with mushrooms. Sprinkle with cheese. Bake 6 minutes or until cheese melts. To serve, cut pizza into squares. Yield: 4 servings.

Serve with: fresh veggies with fat-free ranch dressing

Chocolate Chip Frozen Yogurt (page 25)

Fresh Tomato Pizza
with Gorgonzola Cheese <small>photo, page 61</small>

You just can't beat the taste of ripe summer tomatoes—especially on pizza.

1 (10-ounce) thin-crust Italian pizza crust (such as Boboli)
Olive oil-flavored cooking spray
4 plum tomatoes, thinly sliced
½ red onion, thinly sliced
½ cup (2 ounces) crumbled Gorgonzola cheese or blue cheese
¼ cup chopped fresh basil or oregano

1. Preheat oven to 425°.

2. Place pizza crust on an ungreased baking sheet or pizza pan; coat crust with cooking spray. Top with tomato and remaining ingredients. Bake at 425° for 7 to 8 minutes or until cheese melts. Cut into wedges, and serve immediately. Yield: 4 servings.

Serve with: Crunchy Radish-Cauliflower Salad (page 137)

POINTS:
6

exchanges:
2 Starch
1 Vegetable
1 High-Fat Meat

per serving:
Calories 279
Carbohydrate 36.4g
Fat 9.5g (saturated 2.7g)
Fiber 2.1g
Protein 11.5g
Cholesterol 11mg
Sodium 592mg
Calcium 283mg
Iron 2.3mg

Summer Squash over Polenta

**For an added kick of spice, substitute a flavored polenta
such as sun-dried tomato flavor or Mexican flavor.**

POINTS:

4

exchanges:

1 Starch

2 Vegetable

1½ Fat

per serving:

Calories 205

Carbohydrate 22.9g

Fat 7.7g (saturated 3.4g)

Fiber 4.3g

Protein 10.4g

Cholesterol 12mg

Sodium 597mg

Calcium 251mg

Iron 1.8mg

Garlic-flavored cooking spray

1   (16-ounce) package refrigerated polenta,
      cut into 12 slices

2   tablespoons commercial pesto

2   tablespoons water

2   cups sliced yellow squash

2   cups sliced zucchini

1   (7-ounce) bottle roasted red bell peppers, drained and cut into strips

½   cup (2 ounces) grated fresh Parmesan cheese

1. Preheat broiler.

2. Place polenta slices on a baking sheet coated with cooking spray. Broil 5 minutes on each side or until lightly browned.

3. While polenta bakes, coat a large nonstick skillet with cooking spray; place skillet over medium-high heat until hot. Add pesto and water, stirring well. Add squash and zucchini; cover and cook 5 minutes or until vegetables are tender. Add red peppers; cook until thoroughly heated. To serve, spoon zucchini mixture evenly over polenta, and sprinkle with cheese. Yield: 4 servings.

Serve with: warm focaccia or French bread

meats

✳

Tex-Mex Pepper Steak photo, facing page

No need to spend time marinating—the pungent flavor of the spices quickly coats the steak.

POINTS:
9

exchanges:
3 Starch
3 Vegetable
1 High-Fat Meat

per serving:
Calories 437
Carbohydrate 61.6g
Fat 10.9g (saturated 4.2g)
Fiber 3.7g
Protein 22.4g
Cholesterol 45mg
Sodium 478mg
Calcium 51mg
Iron 4.4mg

2   regular-sized bags boil-in-bag rice
¾   pound flank steak
2   teaspoons chili powder
1   teaspoon ground cumin
¼   teaspoon salt
Cooking spray
1   (16-ounce) package frozen pepper stir-fry
1   (14½-ounce) can Mexican-style tomatoes, undrained

1. Prepare rice according to package directions, omitting salt and fat, to make 4 cups cooked rice.

2. While rice cooks, slice steak in half lengthwise; slice each half diagonally across grain into ¼-inch-thick slices. Combine chili powder, cumin, and salt in a zip-top plastic bag; add meat. Seal bag, and shake until meat is well coated.

3. Coat a large nonstick skillet with cooking spray; place over medium-high heat until hot. Add meat; stir-fry 4 minutes or until browned.

4. Remove meat from skillet, and set aside; wipe drippings from skillet with a paper towel. Coat skillet with cooking spray; place over medium heat until hot. Add pepper stir-fry; stir-fry 2 minutes or just until tender. Add tomatoes; bring to a boil. Cook 2 minutes, stirring occasionally. Return meat to skillet; cook until thoroughly heated. Remove skillet from heat.

5. Place 1 cup rice on each of 4 plates; top evenly with meat mixture. Yield: 4 servings.

Serve with: warm soft flour tortillas
vanilla fat-free ice cream with caramel topping

Tex-Mex Pepper Steak
recipe, facing page

**Grilled Teriyaki
Lamb Chops**
recipe, page 93

Summer Squash Medley
recipe, page 184

Barbecue Meat Loaf
recipe, page 87

Garlic Mashed Potatoes
recipe, page 183

Deep-Dish Pizza Casserole
recipe, facing page

Deep-Dish Pizza Casserole photo, facing page

**Sink your teeth into this meaty, cheesy pizza dish
that's sure to become a new family favorite.**

1   pound ground round
1   (15-ounce) can chunky Italian-style tomato sauce
Cooking spray
1   (10-ounce) can refrigerated pizza crust dough
1½ cups (6 ounces) preshredded part-skim mozzarella cheese

1. Preheat oven to 425°.

2. Cook meat in a nonstick skillet over medium-high heat until browned, stirring until it crumbles. Drain, if necessary, and return to skillet. Add tomato sauce, and cook until heated.

3. While meat cooks, coat a 13 x 9-inch baking dish with cooking spray. Unroll pizza crust dough, and press into bottom and halfway up sides of baking dish. Top bottom of pizza crust with meat mixture.

4. Bake, uncovered, at 425° for 12 minutes. Top with cheese, and bake 5 minutes or until crust is browned and cheese melts. Cool 5 minutes before serving. Yield: 6 servings.

POINTS:

7

exchanges:
2 Starch
3 Lean Meat

per serving:
Calories 337
Carbohydrate 28.0g
Fat 11.4g (saturated 5.2g)
Fiber 1.8g
Protein 30.5g
Cholesterol 58mg
Sodium 926mg
Calcium 202mg
Iron 3.2mg

| **Serve with:** | mixed salad greens |
| | low-fat vinaigrette |

total time ✱ 14 minutes

Ground Beef Stroganoff

Enjoy the rich, homey flavor of classic stroganoff in half the time.

POINTS:

7

exchanges:

3 Starch

3 Lean Meat

per serving:

Calories 367
Carbohydrate 42.9g
Fat 7.6g (saturated 2.4g)
Fiber 3.9g
Protein 31.1g
Cholesterol 98mg
Sodium 611mg
Calcium 93mg
Iron 4.3mg

8   ounces wide egg noodles, uncooked
1   pound ground round
3   green onions, sliced, or 1 cup chopped onion
1   (8-ounce) package presliced mushrooms
1   (12-ounce) jar fat-free beef gravy
1   (8-ounce) carton fat-free sour cream
¼   teaspoon garlic salt
¼   teaspoon freshly ground pepper
1   tablespoon dry sherry (optional)

1. Prepare noodles according to package directions, omitting salt and fat.

2. While noodles cook, cook meat, green onions, and mushrooms in a large nonstick skillet until meat is browned, stirring until it crumbles; drain. Return meat mixture to skillet; add gravy and next 3 ingredients, stirring well. Cook over medium heat 3 to 5 minutes or until thoroughly heated. Stir in sherry, if desired. Serve over drained noodles. Yield: 5 servings.

> **Serve with:** steamed green peas
> hot whole wheat rolls

work time: 8 minutes ❋ cook time: 25 minutes

Barbecue Meat Loaf photo, page 83

Barbecue sauce gives ordinary meat loaf a tangy flavor boost.

1	pound ground round
½	cup barbecue sauce, divided
¼	cup frozen chopped onion, pressed dry
¼	cup Italian-seasoned dry breadcrumbs
2	large egg whites
¼	teaspoon pepper

1. Preheat oven to 375°.

2. Combine meat, ¼ cup barbecue sauce, onion, breadcrumbs, egg whites, and pepper in a large bowl; stir well.

3. Shape mixture into a 7 x 5-inch loaf on a rack in a roasting pan. Spread remaining ¼ cup barbecue sauce over loaf. Bake at 375° for 25 minutes or to desired degree of doneness. Yield: 4 servings.

Serve with: Garlic Mashed Potatoes (page 183)
steamed baby carrots

POINTS:
5

exchanges:
1 Starch
3 Lean Meat

per serving:
Calories 228
Carbohydrate 10.4g
Fat 7.6g (saturated 2.6g)
Fiber 0.5g
Protein 27.7g
Cholesterol 70mg
Sodium 535mg
Calcium 22mg
Iron 2.9mg

Chili-Corn Bread Pie

It's easy as pie—saucy chili topped with melted cheese and warm corn bread all in one pan.

POINTS:
5

exchanges:
2 Starch
1 Vegetable
1 High-Fat Meat

per serving:
Calories 270
Carbohydrate 39.5g
Fat 7.3g (saturated 2.7g)
Fiber 3.5g
Protein 13.7g
Cholesterol 13mg
Sodium 798mg
Calcium 169mg
Iron 2.2mg

Cooking spray
1 onion, chopped
1 (15-ounce) can low-fat chili beef soup
1 (11-ounce) can Mexican-style corn, drained
1 cup (4 ounces) preshredded reduced-fat Mexican blend or Cheddar cheese
1 (6-ounce) package buttermilk corn bread mix
⅔ cup water

1. Preheat oven to 450°.

2. Coat a nonstick skillet with cooking spray; place over medium-high heat until hot. Add onion, and sauté until tender.

3. Add soup and corn to skillet, stirring well; spoon mixture into an 8-inch square baking dish coated with cooking spray. Sprinkle cheese over soup mixture.

4. Combine corn bread mix and water, stirring just until smooth. Pour batter over mixture in baking dish; bake at 450° for 18 minutes or until golden. Yield: 6 servings.

Serve with: orange sections
fat-free or 1% low-fat milk

Pan-Seared Steaks with Roasted Red Pepper Sauce

Treat yourself to tender beef tenderloin topped with a no-fuss red pepper sauce.

1   teaspoon roasted garlic-pepper seasoning or ½ teaspoon black
      pepper and ½ teaspoon garlic powder
½   teaspoon salt, divided
4   (4-ounce) beef tenderloin steaks (1 inch thick)
Olive oil-flavored cooking spray
1   (7-ounce) bottle roasted red bell peppers, drained

1. Combine garlic-pepper seasoning and ¼ teaspoon salt. Rub both sides of steaks with pepper mixture.

2. Place a large nonstick skillet coated with cooking spray over medium-high heat until hot. Add steaks; cook 2 to 3 minutes on each side or until done.

3. While steaks cook, place peppers and remaining ¼ teaspoon salt in container of an electric blender. Cover and process until smooth. Serve steaks with roasted red pepper sauce. Yield: 4 servings.

POINTS:

4

exchanges:

1 Vegetable
3 Lean Meat

per serving:

Calories 188
Carbohydrate 3.4g
Fat 8.0g (saturated 3.1g)
Fiber 0.1g
Protein 24.6g
Cholesterol 71mg
Sodium 379mg
Calcium 11mg
Iron 3.3mg

Serve with: baked potatoes
              mixed salad greens
              low-fat salad dressing

Beef Stir-Fry with Oyster Sauce

**Stir-frying is one of the fastest ways to cook beef;
the secret is to make sure your skillet is very hot.**

POINTS:

7

exchanges:

3 Starch

1 Vegetable

3 Lean Meat

per serving:

Calories 366

Carbohydrate 47.9g

Fat 6.0g (saturated 2.1g)

Fiber 3.4g

Protein 29.6g

Cholesterol 69mg

Sodium 345mg

Calcium 42mg

Iron 4.6mg

1   large bag boil-in-bag rice
1   pound boneless sirloin steak
Cooking spray
1   teaspoon minced garlic
1   (16-ounce) package frozen broccoli stir-fry vegetables, thawed
¼   cup oyster sauce or Worcestershire sauce

1. Prepare rice according to package directions, omitting salt and fat, to make 3 cups cooked rice.

2. While rice cooks, slice meat across grain into very thin strips. Coat a wok or large nonstick skillet with cooking spray; heat at medium-high (375°) until hot. Add meat and garlic; stir-fry until browned.

3. Add broccoli stir-fry vegetables and oyster sauce to skillet; stir-fry 5 minutes or until thoroughly heated. Serve over ¾ cup rice. Yield: 4 servings.

Serve with: Raspberry Smoothies (page 27)

Italian Pot Roast

**Ready when you are, this flavorful pot roast is better than
the average thanks to Italian seasonings.**

1   (2½-pound) boneless round roast
1   medium onion, sliced
¼   teaspoon salt
¼   teaspoon pepper
2   (8-ounce) cans no-salt-added tomato sauce
1   (0.7-ounce) package Italian salad dressing mix

1. Slice roast in half for even cooking; place in a 3½-quart electric slow cooker. Add onion and remaining ingredients. Cover and cook on high-heat setting 5 hours or until roast is tender. Or, cover and cook on high-heat setting 1 hour; reduce to low-heat setting, and cook 7 hours. Slice meat to serve. Yield: 8 servings.

Serve with: Italian-Style Salad (page 134)
crusty French rolls

POINTS:
5

exchanges:
1 Vegetable
4 Very Lean Meat

per serving:
Calories 223
Carbohydrate 7.4g
Fat 5.8g (saturated 2.1g)
Fiber 1.2g
Protein 33.3g
Cholesterol 81mg
Sodium 473mg
Calcium 7mg
Iron 3.5mg

Lamb Chops with Minted Sour Cream Sauce

Got company coming? Served with steamed baby carrots and crusty sourdough rolls, these lamb chops make a quick and impressive dinner.

POINTS:

6

exchanges:

5 Lean Meat

per serving:

Calories 267

Carbohydrate 2.0g

Fat 11.3g (saturated 4.0g)

Fiber 0.0g

Protein 36.0g

Cholesterol 108mg

Sodium 549mg

Calcium 63mg

Iron 1.5mg

¼ cup fat-free sour cream

⅛ teaspoon salt

½ teaspoon dried mint leaves

4 (4-ounce) lamb loin chops (1 inch thick)

¼ teaspoon salt

¼ teaspoon roasted garlic-pepper seasoning or
    ⅛ teaspoon black pepper and ⅛ teaspoon garlic powder

Cooking spray

1. Combine first 3 ingredients; stir well, and set aside.

2. Trim fat from chops; sprinkle chops with ¼ teaspoon salt and garlic-pepper seasoning.

3. Coat a large nonstick skillet with cooking spray; place over medium-high heat until hot. Add chops. Cook 3 to 4 minutes on each side or until browned. Reduce heat to medium-low; cook 2 to 3 minutes on each side or to desired degree of doneness. Serve with sour cream sauce. Yield: 2 servings (serving size: 2 lamb chops).

Serve with: Lemon Carrots (page 180)
sourdough rolls

---

work time: 3 minutes ✸ **marinate:** 8 hours ✸ **cook time:** 16 minutes

Grilled Teriyaki Lamb Chops photo, page 82

A super-easy marinade infuses the lamb with great flavor while you relax.

4	(5-ounce) lamb loin chops (1½ inches thick)
½	cup chopped onion
½	cup low-sodium teriyaki sauce
1	teaspoon minced garlic
Cooking spray	

1. Trim fat from chops; place chops in a heavy-duty, zip-top plastic bag. Add onion, teriyaki sauce, and garlic to bag. Seal bag, and marinate in refrigerator at least 8 hours, turning bag occasionally.

2. Remove chops from marinade, reserving marinade. Place marinade in a small saucepan; bring to a boil. Remove from heat, and set aside.

3. Prepare grill.

4. Place chops on grill rack coated with cooking spray; cover and grill 8 minutes on each side or to desired degree of doneness, basting occasionally with marinade. Yield: 4 servings.

Serve with: hot cooked couscous
Summer Squash Medley (page 184)

POINTS:

4

exchanges:

½ Starch
3 Lean Meat

per serving:

Calories 192
Carbohydrate 8.0g
Fat 7.0g (saturated 2.5g)
Fiber 0.4g
Protein 22.4g
Cholesterol 67mg
Sodium 700mg
Calcium 15mg
Iron 1.5mg

Teriyaki-Ginger Pork Tenderloin

Ginger and pineapple juice spice up this lean pork tenderloin.

POINTS:
3

exchanges:
½ Starch
3 Very Lean Meat

per serving:
Calories 161
Carbohydrate 7.8g
Fat 3.0g (saturated 1.0g)
Fiber 0.1g
Protein 24.3g
Cholesterol 74mg
Sodium 293mg
Calcium 14mg
Iron 1.5mg

1   (1-pound) pork tenderloin, trimmed
    Cooking spray
1½ tablespoons roasted garlic or regular teriyaki sauce
1½ teaspoons cornstarch
¼   teaspoon ground ginger
1   (6-ounce) can pineapple juice

1. Cut tenderloin into ½-inch-thick slices; flatten slices with palm of hand. Coat a large nonstick skillet with cooking spray; place over medium-high heat until hot. Add pork, and cook 3 minutes on each side or until browned.

2. Combine teriyaki sauce and remaining 3 ingredients, stirring well. Add to pork in skillet. Bring to a boil; reduce heat, and simmer 3 minutes. Remove pork from skillet, and spoon sauce over pork. Yield: 4 servings.

> **Serve with:** Curried Rice (page 188)
> steamed snow peas
> orange sherbet

Honey-Mustard Pork with Wilted Spinach

This hearty one-skillet meal gets its rich flavor from the pork's natural juices.

1	(1½-pound) honey-mustard-flavored pork tenderloin
¼	teaspoon pepper
Cooking spray	
3	tablespoons lemon juice
4	green onions, finely chopped
1	(16-ounce) package frozen leaf spinach, thawed and drained

POINTS:

3

exchanges:

1 Vegetable

3 Very Lean Meat

per serving:

Calories 166

Carbohydrate 5.1g

Fat 5.3g (saturated 2.0g)

Fiber 2.6g

Protein 22.5g

Cholesterol 55mg

Sodium 456mg

Calcium 90mg

Iron 2.7mg

1. Trim fat from pork, and cut tenderloin crosswise into 1-inch-thick pieces. Sprinkle with pepper. Coat a large nonstick skillet with cooking spray, and place over medium-high heat until hot. Add pork; cook 3 minutes on each side. Remove pork, reserving drippings in skillet. Set pork aside, and keep warm.

2. Add lemon juice and green onions to skillet; stir in spinach. Cook, stirring constantly, 3 minutes, or until thoroughly heated. Arrange spinach evenly on plates. Top evenly with pork. Yield: 6 servings.

Serve with: Cranberry Waldorf Salad (page 131)
warm whole wheat rolls

---

work time: 10 minutes ❊ cook time: 4 hours or 8 hours

Barbecue Pork Chops

Come home to a barbecue supper; your slow cooker does all the work while you're gone.

POINTS:

5

exchanges:

2 Vegetable

3 Lean Meat

per serving:

Calories 237

Carbohydrate 12.4g

Fat 8.2g (saturated 2.8g)

Fiber 0.8g

Protein 25.9g

Cholesterol 72mg

Sodium 250mg

Calcium 55mg

Iron 1.6mg

8   (5-ounce) bone-in center-cut pork chops (½ inch thick)

¼   teaspoon pepper

Cooking spray

½   cup thick-and-spicy honey barbecue sauce

1   (14½-ounce) can no-salt-added stewed tomatoes, undrained

1   (10-ounce) package frozen vegetable seasoning blend

1. Trim fat from chops; sprinkle chops with pepper. Coat a large nonstick skillet with cooking spray; place over medium-high heat until hot. Add chops, in two batches, and cook until browned on both sides. Coat a 3½- or 4-quart electric slow cooker with cooking spray. Place chops in cooker.

2. Combine barbecue sauce, tomatoes, and frozen vegetable blend, stirring well; pour mixture over chops. Cover and cook on high-heat setting 4 hours. Or, cover and cook on high-heat setting 1 hour; reduce to low-heat setting, and cook 7 hours. Yield: 8 servings.

Serve with: hot cooked rice

Quick Veggie Slaw (page 133)

Skillet Chops and Rice

The secret time-savers in this dish are 5-minute rice and Italian-seasoned canned tomatoes.

4   (6-ounce) bone-in center-cut pork chops (½ inch thick)

Cooking spray

1½ cups quick-cooking 5-minute rice, uncooked

⅔   cup water

½   cup chopped onion

¼   teaspoon pepper

1   (14½-ounce) can Italian-style stewed tomatoes, undrained and chopped

1   (8-ounce) can no-salt-added tomato sauce

1. Trim fat from chops. Coat a large nonstick skillet with cooking spray, and place over medium-high heat until hot. Add chops, and cook 2 minutes on each side. Remove from skillet; set aside.

2. Combine rice and remaining 5 ingredients in skillet; bring to a boil. Arrange chops over rice mixture. Cover, reduce heat, and cook 5 minutes or until liquid is absorbed and rice is done. Yield: 4 servings.

Serve with: sautéed zucchini and yellow squash
Ice Cream Sandwiches (page 33)

POINTS:
8

exchanges:
2 Starch
2 Vegetable
3 Lean Meat

per serving:
Calories 375
Carbohydrate 42.9g
Fat 8.5g (saturated 2.9g)
Fiber 2.2g
Protein 29.5g
Cholesterol 71mg
Sodium 352mg
Calcium 49mg
Iron 2.3mg

Balsamic Pork Chops photo, page 3

**A staple in the Italian pantry, balsamic vinegar guarantees
that these pork chops will be some of the most flavorful you'll ever eat.**

POINTS:

5

exchanges:

3 Lean Meat

per serving:

Calories 210

Carbohydrate 0.9g

Fat 11.4g (saturated 3.8g)

Fiber 0.1g

Protein 24.3g

Cholesterol 77mg

Sodium 178mg

Calcium 31mg

Iron 1.1mg

4   (4-ounce) boneless center-cut pork loin chops (½ inch thick)

1   teaspoon salt-free lemon-herb seasoning

Cooking spray

½   cup balsamic vinegar

⅓   cup fat-free, less-sodium chicken broth

1. Trim fat from chops. Sprinkle chops evenly on both sides with seasoning. Coat a medium nonstick skillet with cooking spray; place over medium-high heat until hot. Add chops, and cook 3 to 4 minutes on each side or until lightly browned. Remove chops from skillet, and keep warm.

2. Wipe drippings from skillet with a paper towel. Combine vinegar and broth in skillet. Cook over medium-high heat until mixture is reduced to a thin sauce (about 5 to 6 minutes), stirring occasionally. Spoon sauce over chops. Yield: 4 servings.

> **Serve with:** hot cooked couscous
> Roasted Asparagus (page 178)

total time ✳ 17 minutes

Glazed Pork Chops

The unique combination of savory sage, sweet currant jelly, and sharp Dijon mustard makes these chops hard to resist.

4   (4-ounce) boneless center-cut pork loin chops (½ inch thick)
Cooking spray
⅛   teaspoon ground sage
½   teaspoon salt
¼   teaspoon pepper
¼   cup minced onion
¼   cup currant jelly
1½ teaspoons Dijon mustard

POINTS:
5

exchanges:
1 Starch
3 Lean Meat

per serving:
Calories 239
Carbohydrate 14.4g
Fat 8.4g (saturated 2.8g)
Fiber 0.3g
Protein 25.2g
Cholesterol 71mg
Sodium 431mg
Calcium 30mg
Iron 0.7mg

1. Trim fat from chops. Coat a large nonstick skillet with cooking spray; place over high heat until hot. Sprinkle chops with sage, salt, and pepper; add to skillet, and cook 1 minute on each side. Reduce heat to medium; cook chops 4 to 5 minutes on each side or until done. Transfer chops to a serving platter; keep warm.

2. Add onion to skillet; cook over medium heat 2 minutes, stirring often. Reduce heat; add jelly and mustard, and simmer 2 minutes or until glaze is reduced to ¼ cup. To serve, spoon glaze over chops. Yield: 4 servings.

Serve with: steamed green beans
crusty French rolls
Raspberry Trifle (page 36)

Pork Chops with Dijon Cream Sauce

You'll never believe that this rich cream sauce is fat-free.

POINTS:
5

exchanges:
3 Lean Meat

per serving:
Calories 201
Carbohydrate 2.7g
Fat 9.0g (saturated 3.0g)
Fiber 0.1g
Protein 23.5g
Cholesterol 68mg
Sodium 567mg
Calcium 46mg
Iron 0.8mg

4   (4-ounce) boneless center-cut pork loin chops (½ inch thick)
½   teaspoon salt
½   teaspoon coarsely ground pepper
Cooking spray
⅓   cup fat-free, less-sodium chicken broth
1½ tablespoons Dijon mustard
⅓   cup fat-free half-and-half or evaporated fat-free milk

1. Trim fat from chops. Sprinkle both sides of chops evenly with salt and pepper. Coat a large nonstick skillet with cooking spray; place over medium-high heat until hot. Add chops to skillet, and cook 3 to 4 minutes on each side or until browned. Remove chops from skillet, and keep warm.

2. Add broth to skillet, stirring to loosen browned bits. Combine mustard and half-and-half; add to skillet. Reduce heat, and simmer 7 minutes or until sauce is thickened slightly. Spoon sauce over chops. Yield: 4 servings.

Serve with: Steamed Red Potatoes (page 183)

Pork Chops with Peachy Mustard Sauce

Savor the wonderful flavor of peaches by using peach preserves as a glaze on these chops.

4   (4-ounce) boneless center-cut pork loin chops (½ inch thick)
¼   teaspoon salt
¼   teaspoon pepper
Cooking spray
½   cup peach preserves
2   tablespoons Dijon mustard
1   tablespoon water

1. Trim fat from chops. Sprinkle chops with salt and pepper. Coat a large nonstick skillet with cooking spray, and place over medium-high heat until hot. Add chops to skillet; cook 1 minute on each side. Reduce heat to medium; cook 4 to 6 minutes on each side or until done. Remove chops from skillet, and keep warm.

2. Add peach preserves, mustard, and water to skillet; cook, stirring constantly, 2 minutes. Spoon sauce over chops. Yield: 4 servings.

Serve with: Skillet Beans and Tomatoes (page 179)
hot reduced-fat biscuits

POINTS:
6

exchanges:
1½ Starch
3 Lean Meat

per serving:
Calories 287
Carbohydrate 26.3g
Fat 8.7g (saturated 2.8g)
Fiber 0.5g
Protein 25.2g
Cholesterol 71mg
Sodium 460mg
Calcium 35mg
Iron 0.8mg

Apricot-Glazed Ham Steaks

Just three ingredients come together to create a tasty entrée.

POINTS:

3

exchanges:

½ Fruit

2 Lean Meat

per serving:

Calories 127

Carbohydrate 9.1g

Fat 3.6g (saturated 1.0g)

Fiber 0.0g

Protein 15.2g

Cholesterol 40mg

Sodium 856mg

Calcium 7mg

Iron 0.8mg

1 (¾-pound) lean ham

Cooking spray

¼ cup apricot spreadable fruit

¼ cup orange juice

Fresh orange slices (optional)

1. Slice ham into 4 (3-ounce) slices. Coat a large nonstick skillet with cooking spray; place over medium-high heat until hot. Add ham; cook 2 to 3 minutes on each side or until lightly browned.

2. Add apricot spread and orange juice to skillet, stirring until spread melts. Reduce heat, and simmer 5 to 6 minutes or until ham is glazed. Garnish with orange slices, if desired. Yield: 4 servings.

Serve with: Brown Sugar Sweet Potatoes (page 184)
steamed green beans

---

poultry

❋

Grilled Caribbean Chicken

Tart, fresh lime juice tones down the spiciness of jerk seasoning, a Jamaican creation.

POINTS:
3

exchanges:
4 Very Lean Meat

per serving:
Calories 153
Carbohydrate 1.4g
Fat 4.2g (saturated 1.0g)
Fiber 0.2g
Protein 25.9g
Cholesterol 70mg
Sodium 97mg
Calcium 13mg
Iron 0.8mg

4   (4-ounce) skinless, boneless chicken breast halves
2   teaspoons fresh lime juice
1   teaspoon vegetable oil
2   teaspoons jerk seasoning
Cooking spray

1. Prepare grill.

2. Place chicken between 2 sheets of heavy-duty plastic wrap, and flatten to ¼-inch thickness, using a meat mallet or rolling pin.

3. Combine lime juice and oil; brush over both sides of chicken. Rub both sides of chicken with jerk seasoning.

4. Place chicken on grill rack coated with cooking spray; cover and grill 5 to 6 minutes on each side or until done. Yield: 4 servings.

Serve with: Gingered Melon Salad (page 131)
hot cooked rice

---

work time: 6 minutes ❊ **cook time:** 12 minutes

Pan-Glazed Chicken with Basil photo, page 4

When you add basil to on-hand pantry staples, you get delicious chicken—guaranteed!

4	(4-ounce) skinless, boneless chicken breast halves
½	teaspoon salt
¼	teaspoon freshly ground pepper
2	teaspoons olive oil
2	tablespoons balsamic vinegar
1	tablespoon honey
2	tablespoons chopped fresh or 2 teaspoons dried basil

1. Sprinkle both sides of chicken with salt and pepper. Heat oil in a large nonstick skillet over medium-high heat. Add chicken; cook 5 minutes or until lightly browned. Turn chicken, and cook 6 minutes or until chicken is done. Stir in vinegar, honey, and basil; cook 1 minute. Yield: 4 servings.

Serve with: Broccoli Couscous (page 186)

POINTS:

4

exchanges:

3 Very Lean Meat

per serving:

Calories 161

Carbohydrate 4.6g

Fat 3.7g (saturated 0.7g)

Fiber 0.0g

Protein 26.2g

Cholesterol 66mg

Sodium 367mg

Calcium 18mg

Iron 1.0mg

Spiced Orange Chicken

**This glaze gives you a triple shot of citrus
with orange sections, orange juice, and orange marmalade.**

POINTS:

3

exchanges:

½ Fruit

4 Very Lean Meat

per serving:

Calories 155

Carbohydrate 7.1g

Fat 1.6g (saturated 0.4g)

Fiber 0.1g

Protein 26.4g

Cholesterol 66mg

Sodium 227mg

Calcium 22mg

Iron 0.9mg

4   (4-ounce) skinless, boneless chicken breast halves

¼   teaspoon salt

¼   teaspoon pepper

Cooking spray

½   cup orange sections in light syrup, drained and coarsely chopped

¼   cup orange juice

3   tablespoons low-sugar orange marmalade

¼   teaspoon ground cinnamon

1. Place chicken between 2 sheets of heavy-duty plastic wrap, and flatten to ¼-inch thickness, using a meat mallet or rolling pin. Sprinkle with salt and pepper.

2. Coat a large nonstick skillet with cooking spray; place over medium-high heat until hot. Add chicken; cook 3 to 4 minutes or until lightly browned. Turn chicken, reduce heat to medium-low, and cook 2 to 3 minutes or until done.

3. Add orange sections and remaining ingredients to skillet. Cook 2 to 3 minutes or until orange mixture is thoroughly heated. To serve, spoon orange mixture over chicken. Yield: 4 servings.

> **Serve with:** Herbed Sugar Snap Peas (page 182)
> warm dinner rolls

Tuscan Chicken and Beans

Rustic Italian flavor made easy—this 3-*POINT* meal cooks in just one dish.

Olive oil-flavored cooking spray

1   pound skinless, boneless chicken breasts, cut into 1-inch pieces

1   teaspoon dried rosemary, crushed, or 2 teaspoons chopped
       fresh rosemary

¼   teaspoon salt

¼   teaspoon freshly ground pepper

1   cup fat-free, less-sodium chicken broth

1   (16-ounce) can cannellini beans, rinsed and drained

2   tablespoons sun-dried tomato sprinkles

Fresh rosemary (optional)

POINTS:

3

exchanges:

1 Starch

4 Very Lean Meat

per serving:

Calories 193

Carbohydrate 11.0g

Fat 1.9g (saturated 0.4g)

Fiber 3.8g

Protein 29.8g

Cholesterol 66mg

Sodium 586mg

Calcium 46mg

Iron 2.2mg

1. Coat a large nonstick skillet with cooking spray; place over medium heat until hot. Add chicken; sprinkle with rosemary, salt, and pepper. Stir-fry 2 minutes.

2. Add broth, beans, and tomato sprinkles to skillet; bring to a boil. Reduce heat, and simmer, uncovered, 8 minutes or until chicken is done. Sprinkle with fresh rosemary, if desired. Yield: 4 servings.

Serve with: Garlic-Cheese Breadsticks (page 13)

Peach-Glazed Chicken photo, page 119

**Don't wipe the pan before adding the preserves; flavors left by the chicken
blend with other seasonings to create a tasty glaze.**

POINTS:

5

exchanges:

2 Starch

3 Very Lean Meat

per serving:

Calories 238

Carbohydrate 26.4g

Fat 2.7g (saturated 0.6g)

Fiber 0.1g

Protein 26.3g

Cholesterol 66mg

Sodium 95mg

Calcium 15mg

Iron 0.9mg

Cooking spray

1   teaspoon vegetable oil

1   pound chicken breast tenders

½   cup peach preserves

2   tablespoons balsamic vinegar

1   green onion, chopped

¼   teaspoon pepper

1. Coat a large nonstick skillet with cooking spray; add oil, and place over
medium-high heat until hot. Add chicken, and sauté 5 minutes on each
side or until done. Remove chicken; set aside, and keep warm.

2. Reduce heat to low; add preserves and remaining 3 ingredients. Cook,
stirring constantly, until preserves melt and onion is tender. Spoon preserves mixture over chicken. Yield: 4 servings.

> **Serve with:** Sweet-and-Sour Spinach Salad (page 138)
> hot cooked rice

Fruited Moroccan Chicken

**This aromatic dish, loaded with sweet fruit,
goes from skillet to table in less than 10 minutes.**

1	tablespoon salt-free Moroccan seasoning
1	pound chicken breast tenders
	Cooking spray
1	teaspoon olive oil
16	dried apricot halves
½	cup reduced-fat sour cream (do not use fat-free sour cream)

1. Sprinkle seasoning evenly over chicken. Coat a large nonstick skillet with cooking spray; add oil. Place over medium-high heat until hot. Add chicken; cook 3 minutes on each side or until chicken is lightly browned.

2. While chicken cooks, cut apricot halves into slivers. Place in a glass measure; add water to cover. Cover with heavy-duty plastic wrap, and vent. Microwave at HIGH 2 minutes; drain well.

3. Remove chicken from heat; stir in apricots and sour cream. Serve immediately. Yield: 4 servings.

Serve with: Curried Couscous with Walnuts (page 187)
steamed broccoli spears

POINTS:
5

exchanges:
1 Fruit
4 Very Lean Meat
½ Fat

per serving:
Calories 233
Carbohydrate 15.0g
Fat 6.4g (saturated 3.0g)
Fiber 0.6g
Protein 29.0g
Cholesterol 81mg
Sodium 110mg
Calcium 69mg
Iron 1.5mg

Szechuan Chicken and Vegetables

Create your own combo of fresh stir-fry vegetables from the salad bar at the grocery store.

POINTS:

4

exchanges:

2 Vegetable

3 Very Lean Meat

per serving:

Calories 183

Carbohydrate 7.9g

Fat 3.7g (saturated 0.7g)

Fiber 1.2g

Protein 28.8g

Cholesterol 66mg

Sodium 341mg

Calcium 35mg

Iron 1.2mg

2　teaspoons dark or light sesame oil

1　pound chicken breast tenders

¼　teaspoon dried red pepper flakes

1　(10-ounce) package fresh stir-fry vegetables (about 2½ cups)

¼　cup low-sodium teriyaki sauce

1. Heat oil in a large nonstick skillet over medium-high heat. Add chicken, and sprinkle with pepper flakes; stir-fry 3 minutes.

2. Add vegetables and teriyaki sauce; stir-fry 5 minutes or until vegetables are crisp-tender and chicken is thoroughly cooked. Yield: 4 servings.

Serve with: Asian Noodles (page 187)

crispy rice cakes

Buenos Burritos <small>photo, cover</small>

The fiber and protein in these burritos will keep you satisfied for hours.

Cooking spray
½ pound chicken breast tenders
1 cup diced red bell pepper
½ cup salsa, divided
1 cup canned fat-free refried beans
4 (8-inch) fat-free flour tortillas

1. Coat a large nonstick skillet with cooking spray; place over medium-high heat until hot. Add chicken and pepper; sauté 3 minutes. Add ¼ cup salsa; reduce heat to medium-low, and cook mixture 2 minutes, stirring occasionally.

2. While chicken cooks, combine refried beans and remaining ¼ cup salsa in a small microwave-safe bowl. Cover with heavy-duty plastic wrap, and vent. Microwave at HIGH 2 minutes or until thoroughly heated, stirring after 1 minute.

3. Wrap tortillas in heavy-duty plastic wrap. Microwave at HIGH 30 to 45 seconds or until warm. Spread bean mixture evenly down centers of tortillas; top evenly with chicken mixture. Roll up tortillas. Yield: 4 servings.

POINTS:
4

exchanges:
2 Starch
1 Vegetable
2 Very Lean Meat

per serving:
Calories 242
Carbohydrate 37.0g
Fat 1.1g (saturated 0.2g)
Fiber 5.1g
Protein 19.8g
Cholesterol 33mg
Sodium 759mg
Calcium 39mg
Iron 2.9mg

Serve with: Mexican Corn Salad (page 141)

Moroccan Chicken and Lentils

**Turmeric, a spice used in curries, gives this chicken its Moroccan flavor.
Look for lentils in the rice and dried bean section of the grocery.**

POINTS:

5

exchanges:

2 Starch

1 Vegetable

4 Very Lean Meat

per serving:

Calories 299

Carbohydrate 30.2g

Fat 2.1g (saturated 0.5g)

Fiber 10.8g

Protein 40.5g

Cholesterol 66mg

Sodium 749mg

Calcium 53mg

Iron 5.5mg

1   (8-ounce) package baby carrots

1½ cups dried lentils

1½ pounds frozen chicken breast tenders

2   tablespoons minced garlic

¾   teaspoon salt

2   teaspoons salt-free Moroccan rub (or ¾ teaspoon
    ground turmeric, ½ teaspoon ground red pepper,
    and ½ teaspoon ground cinnamon)

2   (14¼-ounce) cans fat-free, less-sodium chicken broth

1. Place all ingredients, in order listed, in a 4- or 5-quart electric slow
cooker. Cover and cook on high-heat setting 5 hours. Or, cover and cook
on high-heat setting 1 hour; reduce to low-heat setting, and cook 7 hours.
Yield: 6 (1-cup) servings.

Serve with: hot cooked couscous
                Toasted Pita Chips (page 16)

---

work time: 5 minutes ❉ **cook time:** 4 hours or 8 hours

Chicken Pepper Pot

Put the ingredients in the slow cooker and head out the door.

2 (16-ounce) packages frozen pepper stir-fry
4 (6-ounce) skinned chicken breast halves
1 (10¾-ounce) can low-fat, reduced-sodium tomato soup with garden
    herbs
1 tablespoon white wine Worcestershire sauce
½ teaspoon garlic salt

1. Place all ingredients in a 4- or 5-quart electric slow cooker; stir well.
Cover and cook on high-heat setting 4 hours. Or, cover and cook on
high-heat setting 1 hour; reduce to low-heat setting, and cook 7 hours.
Yield: 4 servings.

Serve with: hot cooked rice or noodles
              crusty French bread

POINTS:

4

exchanges:

1 Starch
1 Vegetable
4 Very Lean Meat

per serving:

Calories 245
Carbohydrate 19.2g
Fat 2.7g (saturated 0.5g)
Fiber 3.3g
Protein 33.7g
Cholesterol 79mg
Sodium 670mg
Calcium 39mg
Iron 1.9mg

Fruited Chicken and Barley

Slow-cooking these thighs all day makes them extra-tender and juicy.

POINTS:
8

exchanges:
3 Starch
1 Fruit
3 Very Lean Meat

per serving:
Calories 399
Carbohydrate 58.3g
Fat 5.2g (saturated 1.3g)
Fiber 9.7g
Protein 28.8g
Cholesterol 99mg
Sodium 316mg
Calcium 44mg
Iron 3.4mg

1¼ cups pearl barley, uncooked
6   cups water
2   pounds skinless chicken thighs
1   large onion, coarsely chopped
1   (8-ounce) package dried mixed fruit
1   tablespoon salt-free Caribbean spice rub
½   teaspoon salt
¼   teaspoon pepper

1. Place all ingredients in a 4-quart electric slow cooker; stir well. Cover and cook on high-heat setting 4 hours or until chicken is tender. Or, cover and cook on high-heat setting 1 hour; reduce to low-heat setting, and cook 7 hours. Yield: 6 (2-cup) servings.

Serve with: steamed green beans
warm multi-grain rolls

Mexican Chicken Skillet

**If southwestern-flavored cooked chicken isn't in your grocery,
substitute 9 ounces of plain cooked chicken.**

Cooking spray

1   (9-ounce) package frozen southwestern-flavored cooked chicken
     breast strips

1¾ cups water

1   (14½-ounce) can Mexican-style stewed tomatoes

2   cups instant rice, uncooked

1   (8¾-ounce) can no-salt-added whole-kernel corn, drained

1   cup (4 ounces) preshredded reduced-fat Mexican blend cheese

1. Coat a large nonstick skillet with cooking spray; place over medium-high heat until hot. Add chicken strips, and sauté 3 to 5 minutes or until chicken is thoroughly heated. Remove chicken from skillet, and set aside.

2. Add water and tomatoes to skillet; bring to a boil. Stir in rice and corn; top with chicken strips and cheese. Cover, remove from heat, and let stand 5 minutes. Yield: 4 servings.

Serve with: juicy orange wedges
              Mocha Milkshake (page 26)

POINTS:

8

exchanges:

3 Starch

2 Vegetable

2 Lean Meat

per serving:

Calories 402

Carbohydrate 55.5g

Fat 7.7g (saturated 3.8g)

Fiber 1.3g

Protein 27.1g

Cholesterol 40mg

Sodium 767mg

Calcium 239mg

Iron 2.0mg

Speedy Chicken Cacciatore   photo, facing page

This version of an Italian classic cooks quickly in just one pan.

POINTS:
8

exchanges:
3 Starch
4 Very Lean Meat

per serving:
Calories 416
Carbohydrate 47.1g
Fat 6.1g (saturated 1.2g)
Fiber 3.5g
Protein 40.1g
Cholesterol 87mg
Sodium 591mg
Calcium 74mg
Iron 4.1mg

1   (9-ounce) package refrigerated angel hair pasta
    Olive oil-flavored cooking spray
1   (18-ounce) package frozen cooked diced chicken breast
1   green bell pepper, cut into 1-inch pieces (about 1 cup)
1   small onion, cut into 1-inch pieces (about 1 cup)
1   (15-ounce) can chunky Italian-style tomato sauce
⅔   cup water
¼   teaspoon pepper

1. Cook pasta according to package directions, omitting salt and fat.

2. While pasta cooks, coat a large nonstick skillet with cooking spray; place over medium-high heat until hot. Add chicken, green pepper, and onion; sauté until chicken is browned and vegetables are crisp-tender. Stir in tomato sauce, water, and ¼ teaspoon pepper. Reduce heat, and simmer, uncovered, 5 minutes, stirring often.

3. Place ¾ cup drained pasta on each of 5 plates; top each serving with 1 cup chicken mixture. Yield: 5 servings.

Serve with: mixed salad greens
low-fat Italian dressing
French bread

Speedy Chicken Cacciatore
recipe, facing page

Turkey Parmesan
recipe, page 125

Sautéed Green Pepper
recipe, page 182

Peach-Glazed Chicken
recipe, page 108

Sweet-and-Sour Spinach Salad
recipe, page 138

Teriyaki Roast Chicken
recipe, facing page

Orange Rice
recipe, page 188

work time: 5 minutes ❋ **cook time:** 1½ hours

Teriyaki Roast Chicken photo, facing page

**You won't be in the kitchen all day preparing this meal,
so take time to add an Asian flair to your table.**

1   (3-pound) broiler-fryer
1   small onion, quartered
⅓   cup low-sodium teriyaki sauce
1   teaspoon garlic-pepper seasoning
Cooking spray

1. Preheat oven to 375°.

2. Remove giblets from chicken. Reserve for another use. Rinse and drain chicken; pat dry.

3. Place onion in cavity of chicken. Brush chicken on all sides with some of the teriyaki sauce. Sprinkle with garlic-pepper seasoning. Place chicken, breast side up, on rack of a roasting pan coated with cooking spray. Insert meat thermometer into meaty part of thigh, making sure it does not touch the bone. Pour remaining teriyaki sauce over chicken.

4. Bake, uncovered, at 375° for 1½ hours or until meat thermometer registers 185°. Remove skin before serving. Yield: 6 servings.

POINTS:
4

exchanges:
1 Vegetable
3 Lean Meat

per serving:
Calories 170
Carbohydrate 3.0g
Fat 6.1g (saturated 1.6g)
Fiber 0.4g
Protein 24.3g
Cholesterol 73mg
Sodium 271mg
Calcium 12mg
Iron 1.0mg

Serve with: Orange Rice (page 188)
steamed fresh asparagus
Strawberry Shortcakes (page 35)

Chicken Alfredo Pasta

Indulge your craving for creamy alfredo sauce with this 5-*POINT* winner.

POINTS:

5

exchanges:

1½ Starch

2 Lean Meat

per serving:

Calories 225

Carbohydrate 21.8g

Fat 6.3g (saturated 3.0g)

Fiber 2.5g

Protein 20.1g

Cholesterol 56mg

Sodium 612mg

Calcium 119mg

Iron 1.6mg

5½ ounces rotini, uncooked (2 cups)

1   (10-ounce) package frozen mixed vegetables, thawed

1   (9-ounce) package frozen cooked diced chicken breast, thawed

1   cup light alfredo sauce or Parmesan and mozzarella sauce

¼   cup shredded Parmesan cheese

½   teaspoon salt

¼   teaspoon freshly ground pepper

1. Cook pasta and vegetables together in boiling water in a Dutch oven 10 minutes or until pasta is done and vegetables are tender.

2. Drain pasta and vegetables; return to Dutch oven. Add chicken and next 3 ingredients to pasta mixture, stirring well. Cook over low heat 2 minutes or until thoroughly heated. Sprinkle with freshly ground pepper. Yield: 6 (1-cup) servings.

Serve with: Cantaloupe with Raspberry-Poppy Seed Dressing (page 130)

total time ❋ 13 minutes

Wagon Wheel Pasta with Salsa Chicken

Kids love the fun-shaped pasta; adults love the quick-fix meal.

8 ounces wagon wheel pasta, uncooked
1 (24-ounce) jar thick and chunky mild salsa
1 (9-ounce) package frozen cooked diced chicken breast
½ cup (2 ounces) shredded reduced-fat Monterey Jack cheese

1. Cook pasta according to package directions, omitting salt and fat.

2. While pasta cooks, combine salsa and chicken in a medium nonstick skillet. Cover and cook over medium heat 5 minutes or until chicken is thoroughly heated, stirring occasionally.

3. Place 1 cup drained pasta on each of 4 plates; top evenly with chicken mixture and cheese. Yield: 4 servings.

Serve with: Berries and Cream (page 28)

POINTS:
8

exchanges:
3 Starch
1 Vegetable
3 Lean Meat

per serving:
Calories 395
Carbohydrate 51.0g
Fat 6.2g (saturated 2.4g)
Fiber 4.6g
Protein 33.1g
Cholesterol 64mg
Sodium 647mg
Calcium 62mg
Iron 3.2mg

Mexicali Turkey Skillet Casserole

**If you're in the mood for Mexican, this healthy skillet casserole
will be your new south-of-the-border favorite.**

POINTS:

6

exchanges:

2 Starch
2 Vegetable
3 Very Lean Meat

per serving:

Calories 330
Carbohydrate 42.0g
Fat 2.9g (saturated 0.6g)
Fiber 2.7g
Protein 32.5g
Cholesterol 68mg
Sodium 589mg
Calcium 33mg
Iron 2.8mg

4   ounces small elbow macaroni, uncooked
    Cooking spray
1   pound freshly ground turkey breast
1   (14½-ounce) can no-salt-added diced tomatoes, undrained
1   (8¾-ounce) can no-salt-added whole-kernel corn, undrained
1   (1.25-ounce) package 40%-less-sodium taco seasoning mix

1. Cook pasta according to package directions, omitting salt and fat.

2. While pasta cooks, coat a large nonstick skillet with cooking spray; place over medium-high heat until hot. Add turkey; cook, stirring constantly, until turkey crumbles. Stir in drained pasta, tomatoes, corn, and taco seasoning; cook 5 minutes, stirring occasionally. Yield: 4 servings.

Serve with: Gingered Melon Salad (page 131)
                 hot corn bread sticks

Turkey Parmesan photo, page 118

Pounding the turkey until it's thin makes the cutlets cook super-fast.

½   pound turkey cutlets
¼   cup classic Italian-seasoned coating mix for chicken
Cooking spray
1½ teaspoons olive oil
½   cup tomato-basil pasta sauce
¼   cup shredded fresh Parmesan cheese

1. Place cutlets between 2 sheets of heavy-duty plastic wrap, and flatten to ⅛-inch thickness, using a meat mallet or rolling pin. Coat both sides of cutlets with coating mix.

2. Coat a nonstick skillet with cooking spray; add olive oil. Place over medium-high heat until hot. Add cutlets; cook 2 minutes on each side.

3. Place sauce in a microwave-safe dish; microwave at HIGH 1 minute or until heated. Spoon over cutlets; sprinkle with cheese. Yield: 2 servings.

POINTS:

7

exchanges:

1 Starch
4 Lean Meat

per serving:

Calories 302
Carbohydrate 14.8g
Fat 11.1g (saturated 3.4g)
Fiber 1.5g
Protein 34.1g
Cholesterol 78mg
Sodium 894mg
Calcium 223mg
Iron 2.7mg

| **Serve with:** Sautéed Green Pepper (page 182) |
| crusty French rolls |
| white wine |

Orange-Glazed Turkey with Cranberry Rice

This turkey and rice duo lets you savor the flavors of Thanksgiving anytime.

POINTS:

7

exchanges:

3 Starch

1 Fruit

3 Very Lean Meat

per serving:

Calories 389

Carbohydrate 57.8g

Fat 2.0g (saturated 0.6g)

Fiber 7.1g

Protein 30.7g

Cholesterol 68mg

Sodium 165mg

Calcium 27mg

Iron 2.4mg

1   (14¼-ounce) can fat-free, less-sodium chicken broth

1   (3-ounce) package dried cranberries

2   cups instant rice, uncooked

Cooking spray

1   pound turkey cutlets

½   cup low-sugar orange marmalade

1. Combine broth and cranberries in a medium saucepan; bring to a boil. Stir in rice; remove from heat, cover, and let stand 5 minutes.

2. Coat a large nonstick skillet with cooking spray; place over medium-high heat until hot. Add turkey; cook 2 minutes. Turn and cook over high heat 2 minutes or until browned.

3. Spoon marmalade over turkey; cook, uncovered, over medium heat 2 minutes or until thoroughly heated.

4. Fluff rice mixture with a fork; spoon evenly onto 4 plates, and top each serving with 2 cutlets. Yield: 4 servings.

Serve with: steamed green beans
whole wheat bread

Glazed Turkey

Sweet potatoes add a nutritional boost of beta-carotene to this quick and easy turkey.

4 sweet potatoes, scrubbed
1 turkey tenderloin (about ¾ pound)
1 (14¼-ounce) can fat-free, less-sodium chicken broth
2 bay leaves
½ cup apricot spreadable fruit

1. Place potatoes in bottom of a 5-quart electric slow cooker; place turkey over potatoes.

2. Pour broth over turkey; add bay leaves and spreadable fruit. Cover and cook on high-heat setting 5 hours or until turkey is tender. Or, cover and cook on high-heat setting 1 hour; reduce to low-heat setting, and cook 7 hours. Remove and discard bay leaves. Slice and serve tenderloin with potatoes. Yield: 4 servings.

Note: There are usually 2 tenderloins in a package; place the second one in an airtight container and freeze up to 1 month.

POINTS:

6

exchanges:
4 Starch
2 Very Lean Meat

per serving:
Calories 342
Carbohydrate 56.6g
Fat 1.8g (saturated 0.5g)
Fiber 5.1g
Protein 23.2g
Cholesterol 51mg
Sodium 110mg
Calcium 37mg
Iron 2.0mg

Serve with: hot cooked wild rice
apple slices
whole wheat rolls

Turkey Pepperoni Pizza

**Skeptical about turkey pepperoni? Give it a try.
You'll agree with us that it's as good as regular pepperoni.**

POINTS:

5

exchanges:

1½ Starch
1½ Medium-Fat Meat

per serving:

Calories 216
Carbohydrate 22.3g
Fat 7.7g (saturated 3.3g)
Fiber 1.1g
Protein 14.0g
Cholesterol 29mg
Sodium 604mg
Calcium 264mg
Iron 1.8mg

1   (10-ounce) thin Italian pizza crust (such as Boboli)
½   cup pizza sauce
2   ounces turkey pepperoni
1   red or green bell pepper, seeded and cut into thin slices
1   cup (4 ounces) preshredded part-skim mozzarella cheese

1. Preheat oven to 450°.

2. Place pizza crust on a baking sheet. Spread pizza sauce over crust; top with pepperoni and pepper slices. Bake at 450° for 10 minutes.

3. Sprinkle cheese over pizza; bake 2 minutes or until cheese melts. Cut into wedges. Yield: 6 servings.

Serve with: fat-free Caesar salad mix
low-fat oatmeal cookies

---

salads

❋

total time ❋ 5 minutes

Tossed Apple Salad

Sweet, crisp apple balances the tangy dressing.

POINTS:

1

exchanges:

½ Fruit

½ (10-ounce) package romaine lettuce
1 cup diced Red Delicious apple
⅓ cup fat-free balsamic vinaigrette

1. Combine lettuce and apple in a bowl. Drizzle with balsamic vinaigrette; toss. Yield: 4 (1¼-cup) servings.

per serving: Calories 42; Carbohydrate 9.9g; Fat 0.2g (saturated 0.0g); Fiber 1.6g; Protein 0.6g; Cholesterol 0mg; Sodium 268mg; Calcium 14mg; Iron 0.5mg

total time ❋ 6 minutes

Cantaloupe with Raspberry-Poppy Seed Dressing

For an elegant side at your next ladies' luncheon, serve these sweet-tart cantaloupe wedges.

POINTS:

1

exchanges:

1 Fruit

¼ cup raspberry wine vinegar
1½ tablespoons honey
1 teaspoon poppy seeds
1 cantaloupe, cut into 6 slices

1. Combine vinegar, honey, and poppy seeds, stirring well; drizzle evenly over cantaloupe. Yield: 6 servings.

per serving: Calories 51; Carbohydrate 11.9g; Fat 0.5g (saturated 0.2g); Fiber 1.1g; Protein 0.9g; Cholesterol 0mg; Sodium 9mg; Calcium 22mg; Iron 0.4mg

total time ❋ 3 minutes

Gingered Melon Salad

To save time buy precut melon at the grocery store.

4	cups assorted cubed melon (watermelon, cantaloupe, honeydew)
¼	cup pineapple juice
1½	tablespoons honey
¼	teaspoon ground ginger

POINTS:
2

exchanges:
1½ Fruit

1. Combine melon, pineapple juice, honey, and ginger; toss. Yield: 4 (1-cup) servings.

per serving: Calories 89; Carbohydrate 22.3g; Fat 0.4g (saturated 0.2g); Fiber 1.3g; Protein 1.0g; Cholesterol 0mg; Sodium 11mg; Calcium 17mg; Iron 0.3mg

total time ❋ 10 minutes

Cranberry Waldorf Salad

We've lightened this traditional mayonnaise-laden salad by using refreshing cranberry-orange relish.

2	small Red Delicious apples, cored and chopped
¼	cup chopped celery
1½	tablespoons chopped walnuts
⅓	cup cranberry-orange relish

POINTS:
1

exchanges:
1 Fruit

1. Combine apple, celery, walnuts, and relish in a bowl; toss. Cover and chill until ready to serve. Yield: 6 (½-cup) servings.

per serving: Calories 67; Carbohydrate 14.0g; Fat 1.3g (saturated 0.1g); Fiber 1.7g; Protein 0.6g; Cholesterol 0mg; Sodium 6mg; Calcium 8mg; Iron 0.2mg

Bok Choy and Tomato Salad photo, page 153

Enjoy the abundance of a summer garden in this colorful vegetable salad.

POINTS:	4	cups sliced bok choy or napa cabbage
1	3	plum tomatoes, chopped
	1	small yellow squash, chopped
exchanges:	¼	cup fat-free toasted sesame soy and ginger dressing or
2 Vegetable		vinaigrette

1. Combine bok choy, tomato, and squash. Drizzle with vinaigrette; toss. Yield: 4 (1¼-cup) servings.

per serving: Calories 51; Carbohydrate 11.3g; Fat 0.3g (saturated 0.0g); Fiber 2.5g; Protein 1.5g; Cholesterol 0mg; Sodium 112mg; Calcium 86mg; Iron 1.0mg

Honey-Kissed Slaw

Honey-mustard dressing gives traditional slaw a new look and flavor.

POINTS:	4	cups packaged coleslaw
1	½	teaspoon celery seeds
	½	teaspoon pepper
exchanges:	½	cup fat-free honey-mustard dressing
1 Vegetable		

1. Combine coleslaw, celery seeds, pepper, and dressing; toss gently. Yield: 8 (½-cup) servings.

per serving: Calories 34; Carbohydrate 8.0g; Fat 0.1g (saturated 0.0g); Fiber 0.9g; Protein 0.5g; Cholesterol 0mg; Sodium 152mg; Calcium 19mg; Iron 0.3mg

total time ❋ 7 minutes

Quick Veggie Slaw

1	(16-ounce) package broccoli slaw	
1	Red Delicious apple, chopped	
1	green onion, chopped	
½	cup cider vinegar	
¼	cup apple juice	
⅓	cup sugar	
¼	teaspoon salt	
¼	teaspoon pepper	

POINTS:
1

exchanges:
1 Fruit

1. Combine broccoli slaw, apple, and green onion in a large bowl. Combine vinegar, apple juice, sugar, salt, and pepper, stirring well. Pour vinegar mixture over slaw mixture, and toss. Serve immediately, or cover and chill. Yield: 9 (1-cup) servings.

per serving: Calories 60; Carbohydrate 14.7g; Fat 0.1g (saturated 0.0g); Fiber 1.4g; Protein 0.7g; Cholesterol 0mg; Sodium 74mg; Calcium 15mg; Iron 0.6mg

total time ❋ 2 minutes

Zesty Coleslaw photo, page 41

A tasty 0-*POINT* salad just doesn't get any easier than this.

4	cups packaged coleslaw
⅓	cup fat-free vinaigrette

POINTS:
0

1. Combine coleslaw and vinaigrette. Yield: 4 (1-cup) servings.

exchanges:
1 Vegetable

per serving: Calories 27; Carbohydrate 6.1g; Fat 0.1g (saturated 0.0g); Fiber 1.7g; Protein 0.9g; Cholesterol 0mg; Sodium 228mg; Calcium 33mg; Iron 0.4mg

Citrus Salad

Surprise your taste buds when you bite into juicy orange sections coated with vinaigrette.

POINTS:

1

exchanges:

1 Vegetable

½ Fruit

½ Fat

2   cups torn Bibb lettuce

1   orange, peeled and sliced

1½ tablespoons reduced-fat olive oil vinaigrette

1. Combine all ingredients in a bowl; toss well. Yield: 2 (1-cup) servings.

per serving: Calories 61; Carbohydrate 10.2g; Fat 2.5g (saturated 0.2g); Fiber 3.3g; Protein 1.3g; Cholesterol 0mg; Sodium 93mg; Calcium 46mg; Iron 0.3mg

Italian-Style Salad

The rich, mellow flavors of the red peppers highlight the fresh crisp greens.

POINTS:

1

exchanges:

2 Vegetable

2   (10-ounce) packages Italian-style salad greens

1   (7-ounce) bottle roasted red bell pepper strips, drained

⅔ cup fat-free Italian dressing

1. Combine salad greens and red pepper strips. Drizzle with dressing; toss gently. Yield: 4 (1-cup) servings.

per serving: Calories 56; Carbohydrate 11.2g; Fat 0.4g (saturated 0.0g); Fiber 2.4g; Protein 3.0g; Cholesterol 0mg; Sodium 474mg; Calcium 100mg; Iron 2.2mg

Romaine and Tomato Salad

Save yourself some work by purchasing prewashed bagged romaine salad mix.

4   cups shredded romaine lettuce

12   cherry tomatoes, halved

1   red onion, sliced

½   cup fat-free French dressing

POINTS:

1

exchanges:

1 Starch

1 Vegetable

1. Combine lettuce, tomato, and onion. Drizzle with dressing; toss. Yield: 4 (1¼-cup) servings.

per serving: Calories 81; Carbohydrate 18.3g; Fat 0.3g (saturated 0.0g); Fiber 2.1g; Protein 1.7g; Cholesterol 0mg; Sodium 309mg; Calcium 28mg; Iron 0.9mg

Tossed Salad with Feta

The sprinkling of feta makes this basic salad go from casual family dinners to elegant occasions.

4   cups torn lettuce

½   cucumber, chopped

3   ripe tomatoes, sliced

¼   cup fat-free vinaigrette

4   tablespoons (1 ounce) crumbled feta cheese

Freshly ground pepper (optional)

POINTS:

1

exchanges:

1 Vegetable

1 Fat

1. Combine lettuce, cucumber, tomato, and vinaigrette; toss. Sprinkle each serving with 1 tablespoon feta cheese; sprinkle with freshly ground pepper, if desired. Yield: 4 (1¼-cup) servings.

per serving: Calories 68; Carbohydrate 5.3g; Fat 4.8g (saturated 1.3g); Fiber 1.6g; Protein 2.3g; Cholesterol 6mg; Sodium 208mg; Calcium 67mg; Iron 1.2mg

total time ✳ 9 minutes

Broccoli Salad

POINTS:

2

exchanges:

2 Vegetable

1 Fruit

½ Fat

1   tablespoon orange juice
1   teaspoon vegetable oil
1   teaspoon prepared horseradish
1   teaspoon honey
⅛   teaspoon salt
2½ cups chopped broccoli florets
¼   cup finely chopped red onion
2   oranges, sectioned

1. Combine first 5 ingredients. Place broccoli in a microwave-safe dish; cover and microwave at HIGH 2 to 3 minutes or until crisp-tender. Rinse with cold water, and drain. Add broccoli, onion, and orange sections to orange juice mixture; toss well. Yield: 2 (1-cup) servings.

per serving: Calories 129; Carbohydrate 25.9g; Fat 2.8g (saturated 0.4g); Fiber 6.5g; Protein 4.4g; Cholesterol 0mg; Sodium 179mg; Calcium 105mg; Iron 1.0mg

total time ✳ 6 minutes

Cucumber-Green Onion Salad

Cool cucumbers and crisp green onions are bathed in a creamy dressing.

POINTS:

1

exchanges:

1 Vegetable

½ Fat

2   large cucumbers, sliced
1   green onion, sliced
¼   cup light ranch dressing
¼   teaspoon cracked black pepper

1. Combine all ingredients in a medium bowl, tossing well. Cover and chill until ready to serve. Yield: 4 (1-cup) servings.

per serving: Calories 55; Carbohydrate 5.0g; Fat 3.6g (saturated 0.3g); Fiber 1.1g; Protein 1.0g; Cholesterol 4mg; Sodium 154mg; Calcium 49mg; Iron 2.6mg

Crunchy Radish-Cauliflower Salad

This crisp salad is loaded with fiber from the vegetables and beans.

1	large head Bibb lettuce, chopped
1	(6-ounce) package radishes, sliced
1	cup small cauliflower florets
1	(15.8-ounce) can Great Northern beans, rinsed and drained
⅓	cup fat-free vinaigrette

POINTS:

2

exchanges:

1 Starch

2 Vegetable

1. Combine all ingredients in a large bowl; toss gently. Yield: 4 (1½-cup) servings.

per serving: Calories 143; Carbohydrate 26.2g; Fat 0.9g (saturated 0.1g); Fiber 7.5g; Protein 7.8g; Cholesterol 0mg; Sodium 491mg; Calcium 65mg; Iron 1.5mg

---

Spinach-Onion Salad

The sweetness of the vinaigrette balances the pungent flavor of the red onion.

1	(10-ounce) package fresh spinach, torn
½	red onion, thinly sliced
¼	cup fat-free red wine vinaigrette

POINTS:

0

exchanges:

1 Vegetable

1. Combine spinach and onion. Drizzle with red wine vinaigrette; toss. Yield: 4 (1½-cup) servings.

per serving: Calories 41; Carbohydrate 8.2g; Fat 0.3g (saturated 0.1g); Fiber 3.1g; Protein 2.2g; Cholesterol 0mg; Sodium 277mg; Calcium 73mg; Iron 2.0mg

total time ✺ 8 minutes

Sweet-and-Sour Spinach Salad photo, page 119

**A generous serving of this 1-*POINT* salad is great
when paired with the mellow flavors of a pork tenderloin.**

POINTS:

1

exchanges:

1 Starch

1 | (10-ounce) package fresh spinach, torn
1 | cup croutons
2 | tablespoons crumbled bacon bits
½ | cup fat-free sweet-and-sour dressing

1. Combine spinach, croutons, bacon bits, and dressing; toss well. Yield: 6 (1½-cup) servings.

per serving: Calories 77; Carbohydrate 13.5g; Fat 1.5g (saturated 0.4g); Fiber 2.1g; Protein 2.9g; Cholesterol 2mg; Sodium 476mg; Calcium 54mg; Iron 1.5mg

total time ✺ 5 minutes

Balsamic Tomato Salad

Plum tomatoes are ripe and readily available almost year-round.

POINTS:

0

exchanges:

1 Vegetable

4 | plum tomatoes, chopped
2 | green onions, chopped
¼ | cup fat-free balsamic vinaigrette
Cracked black pepper (optional)

1. Combine tomato, green onions, and vinaigrette. Sprinkle with pepper, if desired. Yield: 4 (½-cup) servings.

per serving: Calories 28; Carbohydrate 6.5g; Fat 0.2g (saturated 0.0g); Fiber 1.0g; Protein 0.7g; Cholesterol 0mg; Sodium 207mg; Calcium 3mg; Iron 0.3mg

Marinated Tomatoes

**Fabulous when made with ripe, red tomatoes,
this side salad will quickly become a summer favorite.**

4 ripe tomatoes, sliced	**POINTS:**
¼ cup fat-free vinaigrette	1
¼ cup (1 ounce) crumbled feta cheese	
Freshly ground pepper (optional)	**exchanges:**
	1 Vegetable
	1 Fat

1. Combine tomato and vinaigrette. Cover and chill at least one hour. Sprinkle with feta cheese and freshly ground pepper, if desired. Yield: 4 servings.

per serving: Calories 62; Carbohydrate 4.7g; Fat 4.7g (saturated 1.3g); Fiber 0.8g; Protein 1.5g; Cholesterol 6mg; Sodium 205mg; Calcium 41mg; Iron 0.6mg

---

total time ❄ 10 minutes

Black Bean-Rice Salad

**Double the serving size and you've got a quick,
delicious entrée packed full of fiber and protein.**

1 regular-sized boil-in-bag rice	**POINTS:**
1 (15-ounce) can no-salt-added black beans, rinsed and drained	2
¾ cup salsa	
	exchanges:
	2 Starch
	1 Vegetable

1. Use 1 bag boil-in-bag rice to prepare 2 cups cooked rice. Combine rice, beans, and salsa. Cover and chill until ready to serve. Yield: 4 (¾-cup) servings.

per serving: Calories 150; Carbohydrate 33.5g; Fat 0.3g (saturated 0.1g); Fiber 4.0g; Protein 5.2g; Cholesterol 0mg; Sodium 337mg; Calcium 42mg; Iron 2.3mg

total time ❊ 6 minutes

Beans and Greens

POINTS: 2

exchanges: 1 Starch, 1 Vegetable, 1 Fat

- 1 (10-ounce) package mixed salad greens
- 1 (16-ounce) can no-salt-added kidney beans, rinsed and drained
- 1 (15-ounce) can cannellini beans, rinsed and drained
- 1 red onion, thinly sliced
- ½ cup reduced-fat olive oil vinaigrette

1. Combine all ingredients; toss gently. Cover and chill, if desired. Yield: 7 (1-cup) servings.

per serving: Calories 143; Carbohydrate 22.2g; Fat 3.1g (saturated 0.3g); Fiber 7.9g; Protein 6.7g; Cholesterol 0.2mg; Sodium 250mg; Calcium 47mg; Iron 1.4mg

total time ❊ 5 minutes

Tex-Mex Salad

Serve this vegetarian salad in Tortilla Bowls (page 17).

POINTS: 1

exchanges: 1 Starch, 1 Vegetable

- 1 (15-ounce) can no-salt-added black beans, rinsed and drained
- ¼ cup chopped green onions
- ¼ cup frozen whole-kernel corn, thawed
- ½ cup salsa
- 8 cups shredded romaine lettuce

1. Combine beans, green onions, corn, and salsa. Spoon bean mixture over 2 cups shredded romaine lettuce. Yield: 4 servings.

per serving: Calories 111; Carbohydrate 21.3g; Fat 0.6g (saturated 0.1g); Fiber 4.3g; Protein 6.9g; Cholesterol 0mg; Sodium 103mg; Calcium 82mg; Iron 3.0mg

total time ❋ 5 minutes

Mexican Corn Salad photo, cover

Burritos and tacos come alive when you top them with this salsa-like salad.

2	cups frozen corn, thawed	**POINTS:**
½	cup salsa	1
1	green onion, sliced	
3	tablespoons chopped radish	**exchanges:**
4	large romaine lettuce leaves	1 Starch

1. Combine corn, salsa, green onion, and radish. Spoon mixture evenly over lettuce leaves. Yield: 4 servings.

per serving: Calories 80; Carbohydrate 19.1g; Fat 0.5g (saturated 0.1g); Fiber 2.8g; Protein 3.0g; Cholesterol 0mg; Sodium 149mg; Calcium 18mg; Iron 0.8mg

total time ❋ 5 minutes

White Bean and Tomato Salad

This salad is popular in the Tuscany region of Italy.

1	(15-ounce) can navy beans, rinsed and drained	**POINTS:**
1	large ripe tomato, chopped	1
¼	cup fat-free balsamic vinaigrette	
	Bibb lettuce leaves	**exchanges:**
	Freshly ground pepper (optional)	1 Starch

1. Combine beans, tomato, and vinaigrette, stirring to coat. Spoon bean mixture evenly over Bibb lettuce leaves. Sprinkle with pepper, if desired. Yield: 4 servings.

per serving: Calories 78; Carbohydrate 14.3g; Fat 0.4g (saturated 0.0g); Fiber 4.1g; Protein 3.7g; Cholesterol 0mg; Sodium 350mg; Calcium 29mg; Iron 1.3mg

Greek Pasta Salad

POINTS:

3

exchanges:

1 Starch
1 Vegetable
1 Fat

1 (15-ounce) can cannellini beans, rinsed and drained
1 large ripe tomato, chopped
2 cups cooked penne pasta
½ cup reduced-fat olive oil vinaigrette
2 cups finely shredded romaine lettuce

1. Combine beans and tomato; stir well. Add pasta, vinaigrette, and lettuce, tossing to coat. Cover and chill until ready to serve. Yield: 6 (1-cup) servings.

per serving: Calories 148; Carbohydrate 22.4g; Fat 4.6g (saturated 0.4g); Fiber 3.6g; Protein 4.8g; Cholesterol 0mg; Sodium 374mg; Calcium 31mg; Iron 1.7mg

Couscous Salad

POINTS:

6

exchanges:

3 Starch
3 Vegetable
1 Fat

½ (16-ounce) package frozen broccoli stir-fry vegetables
1¼ cups water
1 (10-ounce) package garlic-flavored couscous
¼ cup fat-free Caesar salad dressing, divided
1 (10-ounce) package fresh spinach, stems discarded and sliced
½ cup (2 ounces) crumbled feta cheese

1. Combine vegetables, water, and seasonings from couscous in a saucepan; bring to a boil. Add couscous; stir well. Remove from heat; cover and let stand 5 minutes or until liquid is absorbed. Stir in 1 tablespoon dressing.

2. Drizzle remaining dressing over spinach; toss well. Spoon couscous mixture over spinach; sprinkle with cheese. Yield: 4 (1-cup) servings.

per serving: Calories 325; Carbohydrate 59.0g; Fat 5.2g (saturated 2.4g); Fiber 4.9g; Protein 14.3g; Cholesterol 13mg; Sodium 980mg; Calcium 173mg; Iron 3.2mg

total time �֍ 14 minutes

Spinach Tortellini with Kidney Beans

4   ounces refrigerated spinach tortellini
1   (15-ounce) can no-salt-added kidney beans, rinsed and drained
2   tablespoons chopped green onions
½   cup fat-free roasted garlic Italian dressing
Curly leaf lettuce leaves (optional)

POINTS:
4

exchanges:
2 Starch
½ Lean Meat

1. Cook and drain spinach tortellini. Place in a large bowl. Add beans, green onions, and dressing, tossing lightly. Spoon mixture onto lettuce leaves, if desired. Yield: 4 (1-cup) servings.

per serving: Calories 204; Carbohydrate 32.8g; Fat 1.6g (saturated 0.7g); Fiber 2.4g; Protein 10.2g; Cholesterol 0mg; Sodium 476mg; Calcium 64mg; Iron 0.7mg

total time ✖ 9 minutes

Lemony Bean and Tuna Salad

¼   cup chopped green onions
1   teaspoon grated lemon rind
1   tablespoon dried basil
2   tablespoons fresh lemon juice
1   tablespoon white wine vinegar
1   teaspoon olive oil
1   cup cherry tomatoes, quartered
1   (15-ounce) can cannellini beans, rinsed and drained
1   (6-ounce) can chunk white tuna in water, drained and flaked

POINTS:
3

exchanges:
½ Starch
1 Vegetable
2 Very Lean Meat

1. Combine first 6 ingredients in a large bowl, stirring well. Add tomato, beans, and tuna; toss gently. Cover and chill until ready to serve. Yield: 3 (1-cup) servings.

per serving: Calories 144; Carbohydrate 15.5g; Fat 2.4g (saturated 0.3g); Fiber 0.8g; Protein 14.7g; Cholesterol 12mg; Sodium 26mg; Calcium 49mg; Iron 2.6mg

Roast Beef and Blue Cheese Salad

POINTS:

3

exchanges:

2 Vegetable

2 Lean Meat

8 ounces thinly sliced, well-trimmed deli roast beef
8 cups packed European-style mixed salad greens
20 cherry tomatoes
¼ cup (1 ounce) crumbled blue cheese
⅓ cup fat-free raspberry vinaigrette

1. Divide roast beef slices into 2 stacks; roll each stack, jelly-roll fashion, and cut crosswise into 1-inch slices.

2. Divide salad greens evenly among 4 plates. Arrange beef, tomatoes, and cheese over greens. Drizzle evenly with vinaigrette. Yield: 4 servings.

per serving: Calories 171; Carbohydrate 12.9g; Fat 7.4g (saturated 1.4g); Fiber 2.9g; Protein 14.9g; Cholesterol 5mg; Sodium 579mg; Calcium 105mg; Iron 2.9mg

Roasted Chicken and Pear Salad

POINTS:

6

exchanges:

1 Vegetable

1 Fruit

3 Lean Meat

1 Fat

5 cups gourmet salad greens
½ cup reduced-fat raspberry vinaigrette, divided
2 ripe pears, cored and thinly sliced
1½ cups shredded roasted chicken breast
2 ounces Gorgonzola cheese, crumbled
3 tablespoons chopped walnuts, toasted

1. Combine salad greens and ¼ cup vinaigrette in a bowl; toss well. Arrange salad greens evenly on each of 4 plates. Top each serving evenly with pear, chicken, cheese, and walnuts. Drizzle 1 tablespoon dressing over each salad. Yield: 4 servings.

per serving: Calories 291; Carbohydrate 23.2g; Fat 14.2g (saturated 3.3g); Fiber 3.3g; Protein 19.3g; Cholesterol 50mg; Sodium 356mg; Calcium 147mg; Iron 1.9mg

sandwiches

Vegetable Panini with Feta <small>photo, page 155</small>

This Italian sandwich is packed full of good-for-you veggies and cheese. It's delicious served with a bowl of tomato soup.

POINTS:
2

exchanges:
1 Starch
1 Vegetable
½ Fat

per serving:
Calories 134
Carbohydrate 21.3g
Fat 2.9g (saturated 1.6g)
Fiber 4.7g
Protein 6.3g
Cholesterol 8mg
Sodium 365mg
Calcium 77mg
Iron 1.1mg

1 (16-ounce) loaf French bread
1 (10-ounce) package romaine salad mix
1 (16-ounce) can no-salt-added kidney beans, rinsed and drained
2 ripe tomatoes, coarsely chopped
½ red onion, thinly sliced
½ cup (2 ounces) crumbled feta cheese
⅓ cup fat-free Caesar dressing
2 tablespoons lemon juice

1. Cut a ½-inch-thick slice from top of bread, and set top aside. Hollow out bread using a serrated knife, leaving a 1-inch shell; reserve soft bread for another use. Set bread shell aside.

2. Combine salad mix and next 4 ingredients. Combine dressing and lemon juice; drizzle over lettuce mixture. Toss.

3. Fill bread shell with lettuce mixture; replace top. Slice and serve. Yield: 8 servings.

Serve with: canned low-sodium tomato soup with pesto-yogurt
✳ To make pesto-yogurt, combine pesto with plain low-fat yogurt. Drizzle over soup.

Hot Beef and Pepper Rolls photo, page 154

Use leftover roast beef or beef from the deli to make these hot homemade subs.

Olive oil-flavored cooking spray

½ pound thinly sliced deli roast beef, cut into strips

1 large red bell pepper, thinly sliced

1 large green bell pepper, thinly sliced

1 large onion, thinly sliced

4 (2.8-ounce) steak rolls, split and warmed

½ teaspoon dried oregano (optional)

1. Coat a large nonstick skillet with cooking spray; place over medium-high heat until hot. Add meat, peppers, and onion; sauté until meat is hot and onion is tender. Spoon meat mixture evenly onto bottom halves of rolls. Sprinkle with oregano, if desired, and top with remaining roll halves. Yield: 4 servings.

Serve with: Cinnamon-Apple Yogurt (page 26)

POINTS:

6

exchanges:

3 Starch

2 Vegetable

2 Lean Meat

per serving:

Calories 321

Carbohydrate 53.8g

Fat 4.8g (saturated 1.9g)

Fiber 5.4g

Protein 21.0g

Cholesterol 27mg

Sodium 958mg

Calcium 98mg

Iron 4.8mg

Philly Cheesesteak Sandwiches

Here's a meat-and-veggie-filled sandwich that requires no chopping or slicing.

POINTS:

6

exchanges:

2 Starch

2 Vegetable

2 Medium-Fat Meat

per serving:

Calories 310

Carbohydrate 41.9g

Fat 8.1g (saturated 3.5g)

Fiber 3.2g

Protein 21.1g

Cholesterol 36mg

Sodium 688mg

Calcium 183mg

Iron 3.8mg

1 (16-ounce) package frozen pepper stir-fry

1 (9-ounce) package frozen seasoned beef strips

2 tablespoons creamy mustard blend (such as Dijonnaise)

6 (2.5-ounce) hoagie rolls

¾ cup (3 ounces) preshredded part-skim mozzarella cheese

1. Preheat oven to 350°.

2. Heat a large nonstick skillet over medium-high heat until hot; add frozen pepper stir-fry, and cook 2 minutes. Add beef strips, and cook 3 to 5 minutes or until thoroughly heated; drain.

3. Spread 1 teaspoon mustard blend on bottom half of each roll. Spoon ½ cup beef mixture onto each roll; top with cheese and top half of roll. Wrap each sandwich in aluminum foil. Bake at 350° for 6 to 7 minutes or until cheese melts. Remove sandwiches from foil; serve immediately. Yield: 6 servings.

Serve with: sliced strawberries
carrot sticks

Chili Bacon Burgers

Steer clear of the drive-thru and make your own burger. The barbecue rub and salsa add a zesty punch that you won't find at a fast-food restaurant.

1   (1-pound) package ground sirloin patties (4 patties)
2   teaspoons salt-free cowboy barbecue rub
Cooking spray
¼   cup fat-free mayonnaise
¼   cup chunky salsa
2   tablespoons bacon bits
4   lettuce leaves
4   (2-ounce) hamburger buns with sesame seeds
4   thin slices sweet onion
4   slices tomato

1. Prepare grill.

2. Rub both sides of sirloin patties with barbecue rub. Place patties on grill rack coated with cooking spray; cover and grill 6 minutes on each side or until done.

3. While meat cooks, combine mayonnaise, salsa, and bacon bits.

4. Place lettuce leaves on bottom halves of buns; place patties on lettuce. Top with onion, tomato, 2 tablespoons mayonnaise mixture, and remaining bun halves. Yield: 4 servings.

POINTS:
9

exchanges:
2½ Starch
4 Lean Meat

per serving:
Calories 402
Carbohydrate 38.9g
Fat 12.0g (saturated 3.4g)
Fiber 1.4g
Protein 32.8g
Cholesterol 100mg
Sodium 541mg
Calcium 100mg
Iron 4.6mg

Serve with: Baked Beans in a Pot (page 179)

Horseradish Hamburgers

Horseradish adds a spicy kick to these burgers that can be grilled or broiled.

POINTS:
9

exchanges:
3 Starch
4 Lean Meat

per serving:
Calories 418
Carbohydrate 45.4g
Fat 10.4g (saturated 2.5g)
Fiber 1.4g
Protein 34.2g
Cholesterol 76mg
Sodium 681mg
Calcium 81mg
Iron 5.2mg

1 pound ground sirloin
¼ cup Italian-seasoned breadcrumbs
1½ tablespoons prepared horseradish
Cooking spray
4 (½-inch-thick) slices red onion
4 (2.25-ounce) kaiser rolls, split and toasted
Mustard (optional)
Ketchup (optional)

1. Prepare grill.

2. Combine first 3 ingredients, stirring well; shape into 4 (½-inch-thick) patties.

3. Place meat patties and onion slices on grill rack coated with cooking spray; cover and grill 5 minutes on each side or until meat is done. Place 1 pattie and 1 onion slice on bottom half of each roll. If desired, add mustard and ketchup. Top with remaining roll half. Yield: 4 servings.

Note: To broil, coat broiler pan with cooking spray; place meat patties and onion slices on broiler pan. Broil 5 minutes on each side or until done.

Serve with: low-fat baked potato chips
low-fat deli coleslaw

Saucy Dogs

These kid-friendly chili dogs make a super Saturday night supper.

½	pound ground round
1	cup chopped onion
1	(15-ounce) can sloppy joe sauce
8	low-fat frankfurters
8	hot dog buns

1. Combine beef and onion in a nonstick skillet over medium-high heat. Cook until beef is browned and onion is tender, stirring until meat crumbles. Drain, if necessary, and return to skillet.

2. Add sloppy joe sauce to beef mixture, and bring to a boil. Reduce heat, and simmer 5 minutes, stirring occasionally.

3. While sauce cooks, cook frankfurters according to package directions. Place 1 frankfurter in each bun. Spoon beef mixture evenly over frankfurters. Yield: 8 servings.

Serve with: Honey-Kissed Slaw (page 132)

POINTS:

6

exchanges:

2 Starch
1 Vegetable
1 Medium-Fat Meat

per serving:

Calories 278
Carbohydrate 36.2g
Fat 6.6g (saturated 1.7g)
Fiber 0.9g
Protein 15.4g
Cholesterol 47mg
Sodium 806mg
Calcium 111mg
Iron 2.6mg

total time �֍ 14 minutes

Asian Chicken Wraps photo, facing page

Enjoy the taste of an egg roll wrapped in a soft flour tortilla.

POINTS:

5

exchanges:

1 Starch

2 Vegetable

2 Lean Meat

per serving:

Calories 256

Carbohydrate 23.8g

Fat 6.2g (saturated 1.3g)

Fiber 2.8g

Protein 24.9g

Cholesterol 54mg

Sodium 451mg

Calcium 50mg

Iron 1.9mg

1	teaspoon vegetable oil
2	cups broccoli slaw
1	cup sliced mushrooms
1	(9-ounce) package frozen cooked diced chicken
⅓	cup fat-free, less-sodium chicken broth
½	teaspoon garlic-pepper seasoning
1	tablespoon low-sodium soy sauce
1½	teaspoons cornstarch
4	(6-inch) flour tortillas

1. Heat oil in a large nonstick skillet over medium-high heat. Add broccoli slaw and mushrooms; cook 3 to 4 minutes or until crisp-tender, stirring occasionally.

2. Add chicken, broth, and garlic-pepper to skillet; stir. Cover and cook over medium heat 3 minutes or until thoroughly heated. Combine soy sauce and cornstarch, stirring until smooth. Add to skillet; cook, stirring constantly, 1 minute or until slightly thickened. Spoon one-fourth chicken mixture down center of each tortilla. Roll up tortillas; serve immediately. Yield: 4 servings.

Serve with: Bok Choy and Tomato Salad (page 132)

Asian Chicken Wraps
recipe, facing page

Bok Choy and Tomato Salad
recipe, page 132

Hot Beef and Pepper Rolls
recipe, page 147

Vegetable Panini with Feta
recipe, page 146

Turkey Barbecue Sandwiches
recipe, facing page

Turkey Barbecue Sandwiches photo, facing page

Celebrate the 4th of July by being free from kitchen duty.

¾ pound ground turkey breast

1 onion, chopped

1 (8-ounce) can no-salt-added tomato sauce

1 (7-ounce) bottle roasted red bell peppers, drained and chopped

¼ teaspoon salt

¼ teaspoon pepper

2 teaspoons liquid mesquite smoke (optional)

4 (2.25-ounce) whole wheat or plain kaiser rolls

1. Cook turkey and onion in a nonstick skillet over medium-high heat 4 to 5 minutes or until onion is tender and turkey is done, stirring until turkey crumbles. Stir in tomato sauce and red peppers; simmer 5 minutes.

2. Stir in salt, pepper, and, if desired, liquid smoke. Spoon turkey mixture evenly onto bottom halves of rolls, and top with remaining roll halves. Yield: 4 servings.

Serve with: Vegetable Crudités (page 186)
low-fat baked potato chips or low-fat deli potato salad

POINTS:
7

exchanges:
3 Starch
3 Very Lean Meat

per serving:
Calories 346
Carbohydrate 45.6g
Fat 5.2g (saturated 0.5g)
Fiber 1.9g
Protein 28.1g
Cholesterol 51mg
Sodium 665mg
Calcium 88mg
Iron 3.2mg

Taco Chicken Tortilla Wraps

**Enjoy these Mexican-style wrapped sandwiches for dinner
and for a quick lunch-to-go the next day.**

POINTS:

6

exchanges:

2 Starch

1 Vegetable

3 Very Lean Meat

per serving:

Calories 299

Carbohydrate 36.3g

Fat 1.8g (saturated 0.4g)

Fiber 2.1g

Protein 32.0g

Cholesterol 66mg

Sodium 770mg

Calcium 84mg

Iron 2.5mg

4	(8-inch) fat-free flour tortillas
1	pound chicken breast tenders
1	(1.25-ounce) package 40%-less-sodium taco seasoning mix
Cooking spray	
1	cup thinly sliced onion
2	cups shredded iceberg lettuce
1	ripe tomato, chopped
½	cup fat-free sour cream

1. Preheat oven to 375°.

2. Wrap tortillas in aluminum foil; bake at 375° for 10 minutes or until thoroughly heated.

3. While tortillas bake, combine chicken and taco seasoning in a heavy-duty, zip-top plastic bag. Seal bag; shake well.

4. Coat a large nonstick skillet with cooking spray; place over medium-high heat until hot. Add chicken and onion; sauté 6 minutes or until chicken is done.

5. Spoon chicken mixture evenly down center of each tortilla; top evenly with lettuce, tomato, and sour cream. Roll up tortillas. Serve immediately. Yield: 4 servings.

Serve with: Green Chile Refried Beans (page 180)

Greek Chicken Pitas

**Hummus provides a creamy base for chicken strips,
while feta adds a flavorful topping.**

Cooking spray

1   pound chicken breast tenders

1   teaspoon Greek seasoning

½   cup hummus

4   (8-inch) pitas

1   cup torn romaine lettuce

2   plum tomatoes, sliced

1   small cucumber, cut into strips

¼   cup (2 ounces) crumbled basil- and tomato-flavored feta cheese

1. Coat a large nonstick skillet with cooking spray; place over medium-high heat until hot. Sprinkle chicken with Greek seasoning; add to skillet. Cook chicken 6 to 8 minutes or until lightly browned, stirring occasionally.

2. While chicken cooks, spread hummus evenly over pita rounds. Arrange chicken, lettuce, and remaining ingredients evenly on one half of each pita round. Fold pitas over filling; secure with wooden picks. Yield: 4 servings.

Serve with: Balsamic Tomato Salad (page 138)

POINTS:

6

exchanges:

2 Starch

4 Very Lean Meat

per serving:

Calories 314

Carbohydrate 30.9g

Fat 5.3g (saturated 2.6g)

Fiber 1.8g

Protein 33.4g

Cholesterol 78mg

Sodium 751mg

Calcium 118mg

Iron 3.7mg

Cranberry-Turkey Melts

**These cheesy melts are a tasty alternative to the plain turkey sandwich.
Use leftover turkey from Thanksgiving or turkey from the deli to make them.**

POINTS:
7

exchanges:
2 Starch
1 Fruit
2 Medium-Fat Meat

per serving:
Calories 345
Carbohydrate 38.9g
Fat 9.8g (saturated 4.7g)
Fiber 1.1g
Protein 21.4g
Cholesterol 36mg
Sodium 878mg
Calcium 282mg
Iron 1.8mg

2   (6-inch) Italian pizza crusts (such as Boboli)
½   cup cranberry-orange sauce
½   pound cooked turkey breast, thinly sliced and cut into strips
⅔   cup (2.6 ounces) shredded Monterey Jack cheese with jalapeño
      peppers

1. Preheat oven to 450°.

2. Place crusts on ungreased baking sheets. Spread cranberry-orange sauce evenly on crusts. Arrange turkey strips on top of sauce, and sprinkle with cheese.

3. Bake at 450° for 8 to 10 minutes or until cheese melts. Yield: 4 servings.

Serve with: celery and carrot sticks
                    apple wedges

---

soups

Roasted Garlic-Potato Soup

**Here's a sure-to-satisfy soup that comes together in a hurry,
thanks to instant mashed potatoes.**

POINTS:

5

exchanges:

1½ Starch

1 High-Fat Meat

per serving:

Calories 219

Carbohydrate 25.2g

Fat 7.6g (saturated 3.8g)

Fiber 1.0g

Protein 14.5g

Cholesterol 22mg

Sodium 609mg

Calcium 353mg

Iron 0.0mg

2   cups fat-free milk

1½ cups water

½   (7.6-ounce) package roasted garlic instant mashed potatoes

1   cup (4 ounces) preshredded reduced-fat sharp Cheddar cheese,
         divided

¼   teaspoon freshly ground pepper

1. Combine milk and water in a large saucepan; bring to a boil. Remove from heat; add potatoes, and stir with a whisk until well blended. Add ¾ cup cheese, stirring until cheese melts. Spoon evenly into 4 bowls; sprinkle evenly with remaining ¼ cup cheese and pepper. Yield: 4 (1-cup) servings.

Serve with: Romaine and Tomato Salad (page 135)
            Bagel Chips (page 15)

Creamy Vegetable Soup

This silky cheese soup is an easy way to get picky eaters to eat their vegetables.

1   (16-ounce) package frozen broccoli, corn, and red peppers
3   cups frozen potatoes O'Brien with onions and peppers
1   (14¼-ounce) can fat-free, less-sodium chicken broth or
      vegetable broth
1   cup fat-free half-and-half or evaporated fat-free milk
½   (8-ounce) block light processed cheese, cubed (such as Velveeta
      Light)
¼   teaspoon pepper

1. Combine first 3 ingredients in a large saucepan; bring to a boil. Cover, reduce heat, and simmer 6 minutes or until vegetables are tender. Stir in half-and-half and cheese; continue stirring until cheese melts and soup is thoroughly heated. Stir in pepper, and serve immediately. Yield: 4 (1½-cup) servings.

Serve with: Chili-Onion Drop Biscuits (page 14)

POINTS:
5

exchanges:
2 Starch
2 Vegetable
1 Fat

per serving:
Calories 250
Carbohydrate 39.2g
Fat 3.6g (saturated 2.1g)
Fiber 6.3g
Protein 12.0g
Cholesterol 10mg
Sodium 643mg
Calcium 258mg
Iron 0.7mg

Tomato-Cheese Ravioli Soup

Italian seasonings flavor this pasta-based soup that's even better the next day.

POINTS:
7

exchanges:
3 Starch
1 Medium-Fat Meat

per serving:
Calories 317
Carbohydrate 47.9g
Fat 6.3g (saturated 2.0g)
Fiber 0.7g
Protein 14.6g
Cholesterol 39mg
Sodium 653mg
Calcium 234mg
Iron 1.6mg

1   (14½-ounce) can stewed tomatoes
1   (14¼-ounce) can fat-free, less-sodium chicken broth or
      vegetable broth
½   teaspoon dried Italian seasoning
3   cups frozen cheese ravioli or fresh cheese tortellini (about 12 ounces)
1   small zucchini, sliced
¼   teaspoon freshly ground pepper

1. Combine first 3 ingredients in a large saucepan; bring to a boil. Cover, reduce heat, and simmer 5 minutes. Add ravioli, zucchini, and pepper; bring to a boil. Cover, reduce heat, and simmer 7 to 8 minutes or until pasta and zucchini are tender. Yield: 4 (1¼-cup) servings.

Serve with: low-fat crackers

Chunky Shrimp Gazpacho photo, page 176

Don't let its heartiness fool you. This make-ahead soup is a great low-*POINT* option.

3	cups water
1	pound peeled and deveined fresh shrimp
½	red onion
1	small yellow squash
1	green bell pepper
3	(14-ounce) cans no-salt-added diced tomatoes
1	teaspoon herbes de Provence or ½ teaspoon dried thyme and ½ teaspoon dried tarragon
3	tablespoons picante sauce

1. Bring 3 cups water to a boil in a saucepan. Add shrimp; cook 3 to 5 minutes or until shrimp turn pink. Drain and rinse under cold water.

2. While shrimp cook, chop onion, squash, and pepper; place in a large bowl. Add cooked shrimp, tomatoes, herbs, and picante sauce to vegetable mixture, stirring well. Cover and chill at least 10 minutes. Yield: 4 (1¾-cup) servings.

Serve with: focaccia wedges

POINTS:

2

exchanges:
1 Starch
1 Vegetable
2 Very Lean Meat

per serving:
Calories 161
Carbohydrate 18.7g
Fat 0.9g (saturated 0.2g)
Fiber 6.1g
Protein 20.4g
Cholesterol 161mg
Sodium 387mg
Calcium 97mg
Iron 3.8mg

Beef and Black Bean Chili

Black beans and salsa give a Mexican twist to a traditional winter weather favorite.

POINTS:

4

exchanges:

2 Starch

2 Lean Meat

per serving:

Calories 236

Carbohydrate 27.6g

Fat 3.9g (saturated 1.3g)

Fiber 5.2g

Protein 22.8g

Cholesterol 38mg

Sodium 564mg

Calcium 53mg

Iron 3.6mg

1 pound ground round

2 (15-ounce) cans no-salt-added black beans, undrained

1 cup medium or hot chunky salsa

2 (8-ounce) cans no-salt-added tomato sauce

1 tablespoon chili seasoning mix

Low-fat sour cream (optional)

Shredded reduced-fat Cheddar cheese (optional)

1. Cook meat in a large saucepan over medium-high heat until meat is browned, stirring until it crumbles. Drain, if necessary.

2. While meat cooks, drain and mash 1 can of beans. Add mashed beans, undrained beans, salsa, tomato sauce, and seasoning mix to saucepan; stir well. Cook over medium heat 10 minutes or until thoroughly heated.

3. Spoon into serving bowls. If desired, top with sour cream and shredded cheese. Yield: 7 (1-cup) servings.

Serve with: low-fat tortilla chips

fresh pineapple slices

---

work time: 5 minutes ❋ **cook time:** 4 hours or 8 hours

Chili Grande

Impress guests by serving this meaty chili in easy-to-make Tortilla Bowls.

¾ pound beef stew meat, cut into ½-inch pieces
1 tablespoon salt-free Mexican seasoning
2 (15½-ounce) cans chili beans in zesty sauce, undrained
1 (14½-ounce) can no-salt-added stewed tomatoes, undrained
1 (10-ounce) package frozen chopped green bell pepper (about 3 cups)
1 cup frozen chopped onion

1. Place all ingredients in a 4- or 5-quart electric slow cooker; stir well. Cover and cook on high-heat setting 4 hours. Or, cover and cook on high-heat setting 1 hour; reduce to low-heat setting, and cook 7 hours. Yield: 6 (1½-cup) servings.

> **Serve with:** Tortilla Bowls (page 17)

POINTS:

5

exchanges:
2 Starch
2 Vegetable
2 Lean Meat

per serving:
Calories 256
Carbohydrate 38.3g
Fat 4.0g (saturated 0.9g)
Fiber 9.4g
Protein 22.9g
Cholesterol 32mg
Sodium 722mg
Calcium 94mg
Iron 3.5mg

Mediterranean Beef Stew photo, page 174

The juices from the beef give this velvety stew its richness.

POINTS:
4

exchanges:
1 Starch
3 Very Lean Meat

per serving:
Calories 193
Carbohydrate 16.9g
Fat 4.0g (saturated 1.3g)
Fiber 1.5g
Protein 22.8g
Cholesterol 48mg
Sodium 572mg
Calcium 123mg
Iron 3.5mg

2 zucchini, cut into bite-sized pieces
¾ pound beef stew meat, cut into ½-inch pieces
2 (14.5-ounce) cans Italian-style diced tomatoes, undrained
½ teaspoon pepper
1 (2-inch) cinnamon stick or ¼ teaspoon ground cinnamon

1. Place zucchini in bottom of a 3½-quart electric slow cooker. Add beef and remaining ingredients; stir well. Cover and cook on high-heat setting 5 hours or until meat is tender. Or, cover and cook on high-heat setting 1 hour; reduce to low-heat setting, and cook 7 hours. Remove and discard cinnamon stick before serving. Yield: 4 (1½-cup) servings.

Serve with: sun-dried tomato bread

total time ✳ 14 minutes

Creamy Chicken-Spinach Soup photo, page 175

Canned soups are the secret to this soup's creamy base.

1   (9-ounce) package refrigerated cheese tortellini
1   (14¼-ounce) can fat-free, less-sodium chicken broth
2   (10¾-ounce) cans condensed reduced-fat, reduced-sodium cream of
      chicken soup
1   (10-ounce) package frozen chopped spinach, thawed
1   (9-ounce) package frozen cooked diced chicken breast
2   cups fat-free milk
½   teaspoon dried thyme
¼   teaspoon pepper

1. Cook tortellini in a Dutch oven according to package directions, using 1 can broth instead of water. Add soup and remaining ingredients, stirring well.

2. Bring to a boil, cover, reduce heat to medium, and cook until thoroughly heated. Yield: 6 (1⅓-cup) servings.

| **Serve with:** whole wheat bread |

POINTS:

6

exchanges:

2 Starch
1 Vegetable
2 Lean Meat

per serving:

Calories 300
Carbohydrate 35.0g
Fat 7.0g (saturated 3.1g)
Fiber 2.6g
Protein 24.7g
Cholesterol 68mg
Sodium 759mg
Calcium 265mg
Iron 2.0mg

Hearty Chicken-Sausage Soup

Turkey sausage and Cajun-style tomatoes flavor this gumbolike soup.

POINTS:

4

exchanges:

2 Starch

3 Very Lean Meat

per serving:

Calories 240

Carbohydrate 30.7g

Fat 1.6g (saturated 0.4g)

Fiber 2.6g

Protein 23.6g

Cholesterol 52mg

Sodium 471mg

Calcium 68mg

Iron 1.6mg

1	(16-ounce) package frozen vegetable gumbo mixture
1	pound skinless, boneless chicken breast halves, cut into 1-inch pieces
4	ounces turkey kielbasa sausage, sliced
1	(14½-ounce) can Cajun-style stewed tomatoes, undrained
1	(14¼-ounce) can fat-free, less-sodium chicken broth
2	teaspoons salt-free extra-spicy seasoning
2	cups cooked long-grain rice, cooked without salt or fat

1. Place first 6 ingredients in a 3½-quart electric slow cooker; stir well. Cover and cook on high-heat setting 4 hours. Or, cover and cook on high-heat setting 1 hour; reduce to low-heat setting, and cook 7 hours. Stir in cooked rice during last 30 minutes of cooking time. Yield: 6 (1¼-cup) servings.

Serve with: crusty French bread   Caramel-Banana Sundaes (page 30)

work time: 5 minutes ❄ cook time: 25 minutes

Turkey-Vegetable Soup

Get the homemade taste of freshly chopped vegetables from a package of frozen soup mix.

Cooking spray
1   pound ground turkey
2   (14¼-ounce) cans no-salt-added beef broth, divided
¼   cup all-purpose flour
1   (14½-ounce) can Mexican-style stewed tomatoes, undrained
1   (16-ounce) package frozen vegetable soup mix with tomatoes
¼   teaspoon salt
¼   teaspoon pepper

1. Coat a Dutch oven with cooking spray; place over medium-high heat until hot. Add turkey; cook, stirring constantly, until it crumbles.

2. Combine 1 cup broth and flour, stirring until well blended. Add flour mixture, remaining broth, tomatoes, and remaining ingredients to Dutch oven. Bring to a boil; cover, reduce heat to medium, and cook 20 minutes. Yield: 4 (2-cup) servings.

Serve with: Pretzel Breadsticks (page 13)

POINTS:
5

exchanges:
2 Starch
3 Very Lean Meat

per serving:
Calories 295
Carbohydrate 29.6g
Fat 4.3g (saturated 1.2g)
Fiber 5.0g
Protein 30.7g
Cholesterol 74mg
Sodium 548mg
Calcium 33mg
Iron 2.1mg

Sausage and Black Bean Soup <small>photo, facing page</small>

The fiber in the black beans helps make a serving of this soup just 2 _POINTS_.

POINTS:

2

exchanges:

1 Starch

1 Lean Meat

per serving:

Calories 109

Carbohydrate 17.1g

Fat 1.2g (saturated 0.4g)

Fiber 3.6g

Protein 9.4g

Cholesterol 15mg

Sodium 868mg

Calcium 38mg

Iron 1.6mg

Cooking spray

6   ounces turkey kielbasa sausage, sliced

1   cup diced green, red, or yellow bell pepper

1   (14¼-ounce) can fat-free, less-sodium chicken broth

1   (15-ounce) can no-salt-added black beans, rinsed and drained

¼   cup picante sauce or salsa

Chopped cilantro (optional)

1. Coat a medium saucepan with cooking spray; place over medium-high heat until hot. Add sausage, and sauté 1 minute or until sausage begins to brown. Add pepper; sauté 1 minute.

2. Add broth; bring to a boil. Reduce heat to low; add beans and picante sauce, and simmer, covered, 5 minutes. Top with cilantro, if desired.

Yield: 4 (1-cup) servings.

Serve with: Speedy Quesadillas (page 66)

Sausage and Black Bean Soup
recipe, facing page

Speedy Quesadillas
recipe, page 66

Mediterranean Beef Stew
recipe, page 168

**Creamy Chicken-
Spinach Soup**
recipe, page 169

Chunky Shrimp Gazpacho
recipe, page 165

vegetables
&
side dishes

Roasted Asparagus photo, page 3

The key to successful roasting is a hot oven, so make sure your oven is fully preheated.

POINTS:　1　pound asparagus
　　　　　0　Olive oil-flavored cooking spray

exchanges:
1 Vegetable

1. Preheat oven to 450°.

2. Snap off tough ends of asparagus. Arrange asparagus in a single layer in a jelly roll pan. Coat asparagus with cooking spray, and bake at 450° for 10 minutes or until tender. Yield: 4 servings.

per serving: Calories 18; Carbohydrate 2.9g; Fat 0.5g (saturated 0.0g); Fiber 1.3g; Protein 1.5g; Cholesterol 0mg; Sodium 1mg; Calcium 19mg; Iron 0.7mg

Lemon-Asparagus Packets photo, page 44

POINTS:　½　pound asparagus
　　　　　1　2　teaspoons reduced-calorie margarine
　　　　　　　¼　teaspoon lemon-pepper seasoning

exchanges:
1 Vegetable
½ Fat

1. Prepare grill.

2. Snap off tough ends of asparagus; place asparagus on a square of heavy-duty aluminum foil. Spoon margarine over asparagus, and sprinkle with lemon-pepper seasoning. Fold aluminum foil tightly to seal. Place on grill rack, and grill over medium-hot coals 10 minutes. Yield: 2 servings.

per serving: Calories 35; Carbohydrate 2.9g; Fat 2.6g (saturated 0.0g); Fiber 1.3g; Protein 1.4g; Cholesterol 0mg; Sodium 38mg; Calcium 20mg; Iron 0.7mg

Skillet Beans and Tomatoes

1 (10-ounce) package frozen cut green beans
½ cup coarsely chopped onion
1 teaspoon sugar
¼ teaspoon salt
¼ teaspoon pepper
Cooking spray
2 ripe tomatoes, cut into chunks

POINTS:
1

exchanges:
2 Vegetable

1. Combine green beans, onion, sugar, salt, and pepper in a large non-stick skillet coated with cooking spray. Cover and cook over medium heat 8 minutes, stirring occasionally. Add tomatoes; cover and cook 2 minutes or until thoroughly heated. Yield: 4 (¾-cup) servings.

per serving: Calories 47; Carbohydrate 10.5g; Fat 0.4g (saturated 0.0g); Fiber 1.2g; Protein 2.0g; Cholesterol 0mg; Sodium 162mg; Calcium 38mg; Iron 0.9mg

Baked Beans in a Pot

Get the taste of slow-cooked baked beans without the wait.

1 (15-ounce) can no-salt-added kidney or pinto beans, drained
3 tablespoons brown sugar
2 tablespoons dried onion flakes
¼ cup barbecue sauce

POINTS:
2

exchanges:
1½ Starch

1. Combine all ingredients in a saucepan. Bring to a boil; cover, reduce heat, and simmer 5 minutes. Uncover and cook 5 minutes. Yield: 4 (¾-cup) servings.

per serving: Calories 128; Carbohydrate 25.1g; Fat 0.6g (saturated 0.1g); Fiber 2.6g; Protein 6.3g; Cholesterol 0mg; Sodium 148mg; Calcium 33mg; Iron 1.1mg

Green Chile Refried Beans

Use these spicy beans to make a quick vegetarian burrito.

POINTS:
1

1

exchanges:
1 Starch

1 (15-ounce) can fat-free refried beans with green chiles
2 tablespoons salsa

1. Combine refried beans and salsa in a small saucepan. Cook over medium heat just until heated, stirring often. Yield: 4 (½-cup) servings.

per serving: Calories 98; Carbohydrate 17.9g; Fat 0.0g (saturated 0.0g); Fiber 4.5g; Protein 6.2g; Cholesterol 0mg; Sodium 441mg; Calcium 37mg; Iron 1.6mg

Lemon Carrots

No scraping or cleaning required! Baby carrots in a bag are clean and ready to cook.

POINTS:
0

exchanges:
2 Vegetable

½ (16-ounce) package baby carrots
¼ cup water
2 teaspoons lemon juice
Lemon zest (optional)

1. Combine carrots, water, and lemon juice in a 1-quart microwave-safe dish; cover. Microwave at HIGH 7 minutes or until carrots are tender. Sprinkle with lemon zest, if desired. Yield: 2 (¾-cup) servings.

per serving: Calories 50; Carbohydrate 11.9g; Fat 0.2g (saturated 0.0g); Fiber 3.6g; Protein 1.2g; Cholesterol 0mg; Sodium 40mg; Calcium 26mg; Iron 0.9mg

Dilled Corn on the Cob

Grilling gives the corn a rich roasted flavor.

4   (6-inch) ears frozen corn
Butter-flavored spray (such as I Can't Believe It's Not Butter)
Minced fresh or dried dill

1. Prepare grill.

2. Coat ears of corn with butter-flavored spray; sprinkle with dill. Place corn on grill rack, and grill, uncovered, 20 minutes or until corn is tender, turning occasionally. Yield: 4 servings.

per serving: Calories 73; Carbohydrate 15.7g; Fat 1.2g (saturated 0.2g); Fiber 2.6g; Protein 2.7g; Cholesterol 0mg; Sodium 13mg; Calcium 0mg; Iron 0.3mg

POINTS:
1

exchanges:
1 Starch

Buttery Snow Peas

You won't believe the butterlike taste a yogurt-based spread can give.

2   (6-ounce) packages frozen snow peas
1   tablespoon yogurt-based spread (such as Brummel & Brown)

1. Place snow peas in a microwave-safe bowl. Microwave at HIGH 3 to 4 minutes or until crisp-tender. Add spread, stirring until melted. Yield: 4 (½-cup) servings.

per serving: Calories 46; Carbohydrate 6.1g; Fat 1.5g (saturated 0.3g); Fiber 2.6g; Protein 2.4g; Cholesterol 0mg; Sodium 26mg; Calcium 43mg; Iron 1.7mg

POINTS:
1

exchanges:
1 Vegetable

Herbed Sugar Snap Peas

Clip whatever herb is available in your garden to season these peas.

POINTS:
2

2 (9-ounce) packages frozen sugar snap peas
1 Butter-flavored spray (such as I Can't Believe It's Not Butter)
1 tablespoon chopped fresh basil or other herb

exchanges:
2 Vegetable

1. Cook peas according to package microwave directions. Coat cooked peas with butter-flavored spray; stir in basil. Yield: 4 (¾-cup) servings.

per serving: Calories 55; Carbohydrate 8.8g; Fat 0.0g (saturated 0.0g); Fiber 1.8g; Protein 3.4g; Cholesterol 0mg; Sodium 77mg; Calcium 98mg; Iron 1.2mg

Sautéed Green Pepper photo, page 118

**Did you know that the brighter a pepper's color,
the more cancer-fighting antioxidants the pepper contains?**

POINTS:
1

1 teaspoon olive oil
1 green bell pepper, cut into strips

exchanges:
½ Vegetable

1. Heat oil in a nonstick skillet over medium heat. Sauté pepper until crisp-tender. Yield: 2 (½-cup) servings.

per serving: Calories 29; Carbohydrate 2.0g; Fat 2.4g (saturated 0.3g); Fiber 0.6g; Protein 0.3g; Cholesterol 0mg; Sodium 1mg; Calcium 5mg; Iron 0.3mg

total time ❋ 10 minutes

Steamed Red Potatoes

These buttery, bite-sized spuds compliment all types of meat, poultry, and seafood.

1   pound round red potatoes, quartered

2   tablespoons water

Butter-flavored spray (such as I Can't Believe It's Not Butter)

¼   teaspoon salt

¼   teaspoon pepper

POINTS:

1

exchanges:

1 Starch

1. Place potatoes in a microwave-safe dish. Add water, and cover.
Microwave at HIGH 8 minutes or until tender. Coat with butter-flavored
spray, and sprinkle with salt and pepper. Yield: 4 servings.

per serving: Calories 86; Carbohydrate 18.9g; Fat 0.3g (saturated 0.0g);
Fiber 2.1g; Protein 2.5g; Cholesterol 0mg; Sodium 155mg; Calcium 9.5mg;
Iron 1.2mg

total time ❋ 10 minutes

Garlic Mashed Potatoes   photo, page 83

½   (22-ounce) package frozen mashed potatoes (about 2⅔ cups)

1⅓ cups fat-free milk

¼   teaspoon salt

¼   teaspoon pepper

¼   teaspoon garlic powder

POINTS:

3

exchanges:

1½ Starch

1. Combine frozen potatoes, milk, salt, pepper, and garlic powder in a
1½-quart microwave-safe baking dish. Cook according to package
microwave directions. Yield: 4 (⅔-cup) servings.

per serving: Calories 141; Carbohydrate 24g; Fat 2.4g (saturated 1.2g);
Fiber 1.3g; Protein 4.3g; Cholesterol 2mg; Sodium 371mg; Calcium 100mg;
Iron 0mg

Brown Sugar Sweet Potatoes

POINTS:

2

exchanges:

2 Starch

1   (14½-ounce) can mashed sweet potatoes
2   tablespoons brown sugar
1   tablespoon reduced-calorie margarine
2   tablespoons orange juice
¼   teaspoon salt

1. Combine sweet potatoes, brown sugar, margarine, orange juice, and salt in a saucepan. Cook over medium heat 5 minutes or until smooth and thoroughly heated, stirring often. Stir in 2 to 3 tablespoons water, if necessary. Yield: 4 (½-cup) servings.

per serving: Calories 144; Carbohydrate 30.2g; Fat 2.1g (saturated 0.3g); Fiber 3.1g; Protein 1.7g; Cholesterol 0mg; Sodium 189mg; Calcium 38mg; Iron 1.5mg

Summer Squash Medley photo, page 82

POINTS:

0

exchanges:

1 Vegetable

2   large yellow squash
2   large zucchini
1   teaspoon dried dill
½   teaspoon grated lemon rind
¼   teaspoon salt
1   tablespoon lemon juice

1. Cut squash and zucchini crosswise into ¼-inch-thick slices. Cook in a large skillet in a small amount of boiling water 3 to 5 minutes or until crisp-tender; drain. Add remaining ingredients, and toss. Yield: 4 (¾-cup) servings.

per serving: Calories 34; Carbohydrate 7.4g; Fat 0.2g (saturated 0.0g); Fiber 3.3g; Protein 2.2g; Cholesterol 0mg; Sodium 149mg; Calcium 40mg; Iron 0.9mg

Zucchini Sticks

**Zucchini quickly goes from a vegetable your kids won't touch
to a fun food they can pick up and eat with their fingers.**

Cooking spray

1   teaspoon olive oil

2   large zucchini, sliced lengthwise into strips

1. Coat a nonstick skillet with cooking spray; add olive oil, and place over medium-high heat until hot. Add zucchini, and sauté 4 minutes or until crisp-tender. Yield: 4 (½-cup) servings.

per serving: Calories 19; Carbohydrate 1.6g; Fat 1.4g (saturated 0.2g); Fiber 0.3g; Protein 0.6g; Cholesterol 0mg; Sodium 2mg; Calcium 15mg; Iron 0.4mg

POINTS:

0

exchanges:

½ Vegetable

Skillet Zucchini

Olive oil-flavored cooking spray

1   teaspoon minced garlic

2   large zucchini, sliced and halved

½   teaspoon salt

¼   teaspoon pepper

1   tablespoon grated Parmesan cheese

1. Coat a large nonstick skillet with cooking spray, and place over medium heat. Add garlic, and sauté 1 minute. Add zucchini; sprinkle with salt and pepper. Cook until zucchini is tender, stirring occasionally. Sprinkle with Parmesan cheese. Yield: 4 (½-cup) servings.

per serving: Calories 16; Carbohydrate 2.3g; Fat 0.5g (saturated 0.3g); Fiber 0.3g; Protein 1.3g; Cholesterol 1mg; Sodium 318mg; Calcium 38mg; Iron 0.5mg

POINTS:

0

exchanges:

½ Vegetable

Vegetable Crudités

Create a quick picnic appetizer—get the veggies from the grocery store's salad bar.

POINTS:
1

exchanges:
½ Starch
2 Vegetable

¼ pound baby carrots
1 cucumber, sliced
¼ pound cauliflower florets
¼ pound broccoli florets
½ cup fat-free ranch dressing

1. Arrange carrots, cucumber, cauliflower, and broccoli on a large platter. Serve with ranch dressing. Yield: 4 servings.

per serving: Calories 85; Carbohydrate 18.7g; Fat 0.3g (saturated 0.1g); Fiber 2.8g; Protein 3.0g; Cholesterol 0mg; Sodium 339mg; Calcium 43mg; Iron 0.7mg

Broccoli Couscous photo, page 4

POINTS:
3

exchanges:
2 Starch
1 Vegetable

1 (10-ounce) package frozen chopped broccoli
1 (14¼-ounce) can fat-free, less-sodium chicken broth
½ teaspoon salt
¼ teaspoon freshly ground pepper
1 cup uncooked couscous

1. Thaw broccoli, and drain. Combine chicken broth, salt, and pepper in a saucepan; bring to a boil. Stir in couscous and broccoli. Cover, remove from heat, and let stand 5 minutes or until liquid is absorbed. Fluff with a fork. Yield: 4 (1-cup) servings.

per serving: Calories 180; Carbohydrate 36.2g; Fat 0.6g (saturated 0.0g); Fiber 3.5g; Protein 7.8g; Cholesterol 0mg; Sodium 399mg; Calcium 51mg; Iron 1.1mg

Curried Couscous with Walnuts

1   (14¼-ounce) can fat-free, less-sodium chicken broth
¼   cup water
½   teaspoon curry powder
1   (10-ounce) package couscous
½   cup sliced green onions
2   tablespoons chopped walnuts

POINTS:
5

exchanges:
2½ Starch
1 Fruit
½ Fat

1. Combine chicken broth, water, and curry powder in a saucepan; bring to a boil. Stir in couscous; cover, remove from heat, and let stand 5 minutes. Stir in green onions and walnuts; fluff couscous with a fork. Yield: 4 (1¼-cup) servings.

per serving: Calories 272; Carbohydrate 51.6g; Fat 2.9g (saturated 0.1g); Fiber 3.0g; Protein 10.1g; Cholesterol 0mg; Sodium 92mg; Calcium 22mg; Iron 1.0mg

Asian Noodles

This simple, high-flavor side goes well with pork and beef.

1   (5-ounce) package Japanese curly noodles
½   cup thinly sliced green onions
2   tablespoons low-sodium soy sauce
1   teaspoon sesame oil

POINTS:
3

exchanges:
2 Starch

1. Cook Japanese noodles according to package directions; drain well. Combine cooked noodles, green onions, soy sauce, and sesame oil. Yield: 4 (¾-cup) servings.

per serving: Calories 140; Carbohydrate 26.5g; Fat 1.8g (saturated 0.2g); Fiber 0.8g; Protein 3.9g; Cholesterol 0mg; Sodium 389mg; Calcium 0mg; Iron 0.5mg

total time ❋ 10 minutes

Orange Rice photo, page 120

POINTS:

2

exchanges:

1½ Starch

2   regular-sized bags boil-in-bag rice

¼   teaspoon salt

¼   teaspoon ground ginger

½   teaspoon grated orange rind

Orange slices (optional)

1. Prepare bags of rice according to package directions. Remove rice from bags, and place rice in a serving bowl. Stir in salt, ginger, and orange rind. Garnish with orange slices, if desired. Yield: 6 (½-cup) servings.

per serving: Calories 108; Carbohydrate 24.1g; Fat 0.1g (saturated 0.0g); Fiber 0.5g; Protein 2.0g; Cholesterol 0mg; Sodium 98mg; Calcium 8mg; Iron 1.0mg

total time ❋ 12 minutes

Curried Rice

POINTS:

2

exchanges:

2 Starch

1   regular-sized bag boil-in-bag rice

2   tablespoons raisins

½   teaspoon curry powder

¼   teaspoon salt

2   chopped green onions

1. Prepare 2 cups cooked rice according to package directions. Remove rice from bag, and place rice in a serving bowl. Stir in raisins, curry powder, salt, and green onions. Yield: 4 (½-cup) servings.

per serving: Calories 120; Carbohydrate 26.4g; Fat 0.3g (saturated 0.1g); Fiber 0.8g; Protein 2.3g; Cholesterol 0mg; Sodium 148mg; Calcium 12mg; Iron 1.1mg

Recipe Index

Apples
  Salad, Cranberry Waldorf, 131
  Salad, Tossed Apple, 130
  Yogurt, Cinnamon-Apple, 26
Apricots
  Chicken, Fruited Moroccan, 109
  Ham Steaks, Apricot-Glazed, 102
Artichoke Sauce, Fettuccine with Blue
    Cheese-, 72
Asparagus Packets, Lemon-, 178
Asparagus, Roasted, 178

Bacon Burgers, Chili, 149
Bananas
  Parfaits, Caramel-Toffee, 31
  Splits, Upside-Down Brownie, 38
  Sundaes, Caramel-Banana, 30
Barbecue. See also Grilled.
  Meat Loaf, Barbecue, 87
  Pork Chops, Barbecue, 96
  Turkey Barbecue Sandwiches, 157
Barley, Fruited Chicken and, 114
Beans
  Baked Beans in a Pot, 179
  Burritos, Black Bean, 69
  Burritos, Buenos, 111
  Casserole, Cheesy Bean, 67
  Chicken and Beans, Tuscan, 107
  Chili, Beef and Black Bean, 166
  Chili Grande, 167
  Refried Beans, Green Chile, 180
  Salads
    Black Bean-Rice Salad, 139
    Greens, Beans and, 140
    Spinach Tortellini with Kidney
      Beans, 143
    Tex-Mex Salad, 140
    Tuna Salad, Lemony Bean
      and, 143
    White Bean and Tomato
      Salad, 141
  Skillet Beans and Tomatoes, 179
  Soup, Sausage and Black
    Bean, 172
  Tacos, Vegetarian, 70
Beef. See also Beef, Ground.
  Chili Grande, 167
  Pot Roast, Italian, 91
  Rolls, Hot Beef and Pepper, 147
  Salad, Roast Beef and Blue
    Cheese, 144

  Sandwiches, Philly
    Cheesesteak, 148
  Steaks
    Pan-Seared Steaks with
      Roasted Red Pepper
      Sauce, 89
    Pepper Steak, Tex-Mex, 80
    Stir-Fry with Oyster Sauce,
      Beef, 90
  Stew, Mediterranean Beef, 168
Beef, Ground
  Burgers, Chili Bacon, 149
  Casserole, Deep-Dish Pizza, 85
  Chili, Beef and Black Bean, 166
  Dogs, Saucy, 151
  Hamburgers, Horseradish, 150
  Meat Loaf, Barbecue, 87
  Stroganoff, Ground Beef, 86
Beverages
  Milkshake, Mocha, 26
  Smoothies, Raspberry, 27
Biscuits, Chili-Onion Drop, 14
Bok Choy and Tomato Salad, 132
Breads. See also specific types.
  Bagel Chips, 15
  Breadsticks, Garlic-Cheese, 13
  Breadsticks, Pretzel, 13
  Garlic Bread, 12
  Pita Chips, Toasted, 16
  Pita Wedges, Zesty, 16
  Rolls, Garlic-Dill, 14
  Toasts, Parmesan, 12
  Tortilla Bowls, 17
  Tortilla Wedges, 17
  Waffle Crisps, Cinnamon, 18
  Won Ton Crisps, Baked, 18
Broccoli
  Couscous, Broccoli, 186
  Salad, Broccoli, 136
  Tortellini Primavera with Pesto
    Sauce, 74
Burritos, Black Bean, 69
Burritos, Buenos, 111

Cakes
  Brownie Cakes, Individual, 38
  Shortcakes, Raspberry, 36
  Shortcakes, Strawberry, 35
  Shortcakes, Strawberry-Waffle, 32
Caramel-Banana Sundaes, 30
Caramel-Toffee Parfaits, 31

Carrots, Lemon, 180
Casseroles
  Bean Casserole, Cheesy, 67
  Pizza Casserole, Deep-Dish, 85
  Turkey Skillet Casserole,
    Mexicali, 124
  Vegetable Bake, Southwestern, 68
Cauliflower Salad, Crunchy Radish-, 137
Cheese
  Breadsticks, Garlic-Cheese, 13
  Casserole, Cheesy Bean, 67
  Casserole, Deep-Dish Pizza, 85
  Chicken Skillet, Mexican, 115
  Grouper Athenian, 47
  Omelet, Confetti Cheese, 71
  Pizza, Turkey Pepperoni, 128
  Pizza with Gorgonzola Cheese,
    Fresh Tomato, 77
  Quesadillas, Speedy, 66
  Salad, Roast Beef and Blue
    Cheese, 144
  Salad with Feta, Tossed, 135
  Sandwiches
    Melts, Cranberry-Turkey, 160
    Panini with Feta,
      Vegetable, 146
    Philly Cheesesteak
      Sandwiches, 148
    Pitas, Greek Chicken, 159
  Sauce, Fettuccine with Blue
    Cheese-Artichoke, 72
  Soups
    Roasted Garlic-Potato
      Soup, 162
    Tomato-Cheese Ravioli
      Soup, 164
    Vegetable Soup, Creamy, 163
  Tacos, Vegetarian, 70
  Toasts, Parmesan, 12
  Turkey Parmesan, 125
  Ziti and Vegetables, Skillet, 75
Chicken
  Burritos, Buenos, 111
  Cacciatore, Speedy Chicken, 116
  Fruited Chicken and Barley, 114
  Glazed Chicken, Peach-, 108
  Glazed Chicken with Basil, Pan-, 105
  Grilled Caribbean Chicken, 104
  Mexican Chicken Skillet, 115
  Moroccan Chicken and Lentils, 112
  Moroccan Chicken, Fruited, 109
  Pasta, Chicken Alfredo, 122

Pepper Pot, Chicken, 113
Roast Chicken, Teriyaki, 121
Salad, Roasted Chicken and
    Pear, 144
Salsa Chicken, Wagon Wheel Pasta
    with, 123
Sandwiches
        Pitas, Greek Chicken, 159
        Wraps, Asian Chicken, 152
        Wraps, Taco Chicken
            Tortilla, 158
Soup, Creamy Chicken-
    Spinach, 169
Soup, Hearty Chicken-
    Sausage, 170
Spiced Orange Chicken, 106
Szechuan Chicken and
    Vegetables, 110
Tuscan Chicken and Beans, 107
Chili, Beef and Black Bean, 166
Chili Grande, 167
Chocolate
    Brownie Cakes, Individual, 38
    Brownie Splits, Upside-Down, 38
    Brownie Sundae for One, 37
    Brownie Torte, 38
    Ice Cream Sandwiches, 33
    Milkshake, Mocha, 26
    Parfaits, Chocolate-Peppermint, 31
    Pie, Chocolate-Peanut Butter, 35
    Pie, Frozen Chocolate, 34
    Sundaes, Neapolitan, 30
    Wafflewiches, 32
    Yogurt, Chocolate Chip
        Frozen, 25
Clams, Angel Hair Pasta with, 55
Corn
    Cob, Dilled Corn on the, 181
    Salad, Mexican Corn, 141
    Salad, Tex-Mex, 140
Corn Bread Pie, Chili-, 88
Corn Bread, Skillet, 15
Couscous
    Broccoli Couscous, 186
    Curried Couscous with
        Walnuts, 187
    Salad, Couscous, 142
Cranberries
    Melts, Cranberry-Turkey, 160
    Rice, Orange-Glazed Turkey with
        Cranberry, 126
    Salad, Cranberry Waldorf, 131
Cucumber-Green Onion Salad, 136
Curried Couscous with Walnuts, 187
Curried Rice, 188

Desserts. See also specific types.
    Berries and Cream, 28
    Frozen Raspberry Desserts, 34
    Melon Duo, Refreshing, 20
    Parfaits, Caramel-Toffee, 31
    Parfaits, Chocolate-Peppermint, 31
    Parfaits, Raspberry-Lemon, 20
    Parfaits, Strawberry Whip, 33
    Sandwiches, Ice Cream, 33
    Splits, Upside-Down Brownie, 38
    Strawberries and Cream, 25
    Sundae for One, Brownie, 37
    Sundaes, Caramel-Banana, 30
    Sundaes, Honeybee, 27
    Sundaes, Neapolitan, 30
    Sundaes, Strawberry, 29
    Trifle, Raspberry, 36
    Waffle-Fruit Cup, Layered, 29
    Wafflewiches, 32
    Yogurt, Chocolate Chip
        Frozen, 25
    Yogurt, Cinnamon-Apple, 26
    Yogurt, Fruited Frozen, 28

Fettuccine and Shrimp, Zesty, 60
Fettuccine with Blue Cheese-
    Artichoke Sauce, 72
Fish. See also specific types.
    Catfish, Country, 40
    Flounder with Pineapple Salsa,
        Broiled, 46
    Grouper Athenian, 47
    Orange Roughy, Citrus-Jerk, 48
    Orange Roughy, Sunflower, 49
    Red Snapper Vera Cruz, 51
    Swordfish, Cajun-Style, 52
Frankfurters
    Saucy Dogs, 151
Fruit. See also specific types.
    Berries and Cream, 28
    Chicken and Barley, Fruited, 114
    Cup, Layered Waffle-Fruit, 29
    Orange Roughy, Citrus-Jerk, 48
    Yogurt, Fruited Frozen, 28

Gazpacho, Chunky Shrimp, 165
Grilled
    Asparagus Packets, Lemon-, 178
    Burgers, Chili Bacon, 149
    Chicken, Grilled Caribbean, 104
    Corn on the Cob, Dilled, 181
    Hamburgers, Horseradish, 150
    Lamb Chops, Grilled Teriyaki, 93

Salmon, Grilled Honey-
    Balsamic, 45
Scallops and Tomatoes, Grilled, 57

Ham Steaks, Apricot-Glazed, 102

Ice Cream
    Parfaits, Caramel-Toffee, 31
    Pie, Frozen Chocolate, 34
    Sandwiches, Ice Cream, 33
    Splits, Upside-Down Brownie, 38
    Sundae for One, Brownie, 37
    Sundaes, Caramel-Banana, 30

Lamb Chops, Grilled Teriyaki, 93
Lamb Chops with Minted Sour Cream
    Sauce, 92
Lemon
    Asparagus Packets, Lemon-, 178
    Carrots, Lemon, 180
    Parfaits, Raspberry-Lemon, 20
    Salad, Lemony Bean and
        Tuna, 143
Lentils, Moroccan Chicken and, 112
Linguine and Mussels Marinara, 56

Meat Loaf, Barbecue, 87
Melons
    Cantaloupe with Raspberry-Poppy
        Seed Dressing, 130
    Duo, Refreshing Melon, 20
    Salad, Gingered Melon, 131
Mushroom Pizza, 76
Mussels Marinara, Linguine and, 56

Noodles, Asian, 187

Omelet, Confetti Cheese, 71
Onions
    Biscuits, Chili-Onion Drop, 14
    Noodles, Asian, 187
    Pot Roast, Italian, 91
    Quesadillas, Speedy, 66
    Salad, Cucumber-Green
        Onion, 136
    Salad, Spinach-Onion, 137
Oranges
    Chicken, Spiced Orange, 106
    Rice, Orange, 188

Salad, Citrus, 134
Salmon, Orange-Glazed, 50
Turkey with Cranberry Rice,
    Orange-Glazed, 126
Oyster Sauce, Beef Stir-Fry with, 90

Pastas. See also specific types.
Angel Hair Pasta with Clams, 55
Chicken Alfredo Pasta, 122
Chicken Cacciatore, Speedy, 116
Mediterranean Pasta with
    Zucchini, 73
Primavera, Tuna Pasta, 53
Salad, Greek Pasta, 142
Tortellini Primavera with Pesto
    Sauce, 74
Tortellini with Kidney Beans,
    Spinach, 143
Wagon Wheel Pasta with Salsa
    Chicken, 123
Ziti and Vegetables, Skillet, 75
Peach-Glazed Chicken, 108
Peanut Butter Pie, Chocolate-, 35
Pear Salad, Roasted Chicken
    and, 144
Peas, Buttery Snow, 181
Peas, Herbed Sugar Snap, 182
Peppermint Parfaits, Chocolate-, 31
Peppers
Burritos, Buenos, 111
Chicken Pepper Pot, 113
Roasted Red Pepper Sauce, Pan-
    Seared Steaks with, 89
Rolls, Hot Beef and Pepper, 147
Salad, Italian-Style, 134
Sandwiches, Philly
    Cheesesteak, 148
Sautéed Green Pepper, 182
Steak, Tex-Mex Pepper, 80
Pies
Chili-Corn Bread Pie, 88
Chocolate-Peanut Butter Pie, 35
Chocolate Pie, Frozen, 34
Pineapple Salsa, Broiled Flounder
    with, 46
Pizza
Casserole, Deep-Dish Pizza, 85
Mushroom Pizza, 76
Tomato Pizza with Gorgonzola
    Cheese, Fresh, 77
Turkey Pepperoni Pizza, 128
Polenta, Summer Squash over, 78
Polenta with Shrimp and Tomato
    Sauce, 59

Pork
Balsamic Pork Chops, 98
Barbecue Pork Chops, 96
Dijon Cream Sauce, Pork Chops
    with, 100
Glazed Pork Chops, 99
Honey-Mustard Pork with Wilted
    Spinach, 95
Peachy Mustard Sauce, Pork Chops
    with, 101
Skillet Chops and Rice, 97
Teriyaki-Ginger Pork Tenderloin, 94
Potatoes. See also Sweet Potatoes.
Mashed Potatoes, Garlic, 183
Soup, Roasted Garlic-Potato, 162
Steamed Red Potatoes, 183

Quesadillas, Speedy, 66

Raspberries
Desserts, Frozen Raspberry, 34
Dressing, Cantaloupe with
    Raspberry-Poppy Seed, 130
Parfaits, Raspberry-Lemon, 20
Shortcakes, Raspberry, 36
Smoothies, Raspberry, 27
Trifle, Raspberry, 36
Ravioli Soup, Tomato-Cheese, 164
Rice
Chicken Skillet, Mexican, 115
Chops and Rice, Skillet, 97
Cranberry Rice, Orange-Glazed
    Turkey with, 126
Curried Rice, 188
Orange Rice, 188
Salad, Black Bean-Rice, 139

Salads and Salad Dressings. See
also Slaws.
Bean and Tuna Salad,
    Lemony, 143
Beans and Greens, 140
Black Bean-Rice Salad, 139
Bok Choy and Tomato Salad, 132
Broccoli Salad, 136
Cantaloupe with Raspberry-Poppy
    Seed Dressing, 130
Citrus Salad, 134
Corn Salad, Mexican, 141
Couscous Salad, 142
Cucumber-Green Onion Salad, 136

Italian-Style Salad, 134
Melon Salad, Gingered, 131
Pasta Salad, Greek, 142
Radish-Cauliflower Salad,
    Crunchy, 137
Roast Beef and Blue Cheese
    Salad, 144
Roasted Chicken and Pear
    Salad, 144
Romaine and Tomato Salad, 135
Spinach-Onion Salad, 137
Spinach Salad, Sweet-and-
    Sour, 138
Tex-Mex Salad, 140
Tomatoes, Marinated, 139
Tomato Salad, Balsamic, 138
Tossed Apple Salad, 130
Tossed Salad with Feta, 135
Waldorf Salad, Cranberry, 131
White Bean and Tomato
    Salad, 141
Salmon, Grilled Honey-Balsamic, 45
Salmon, Orange-Glazed, 50
Salsa, Broiled Flounder with
    Pineapple, 46
Sandwiches
Cheesesteak Sandwiches,
    Philly, 148
Melts, Cranberry-Turkey, 160
Panini with Feta, Vegetable, 146
Pitas, Greek Chicken, 159
Rolls, Hot Beef and Pepper, 147
Turkey Barbecue Sandwiches, 157
Wraps, Asian Chicken, 152
Wraps, Taco Chicken Tortilla, 158
Sauces. See also Salsa.
Blue Cheese-Artichoke Sauce,
    Fettuccine with, 72
Dijon Cream Sauce, Pork Chops
    with, 100
Minted Sour Cream Sauce, Lamb
    Chops with, 92
Oyster Sauce, Beef Stir-Fry
    with, 90
Peachy Mustard Sauce, Pork Chops
    with, 101
Pesto Sauce, Tortellini Primavera
    with, 74
Roasted Red Pepper Sauce, Pan-
    Seared Steaks with, 89
Tomato Sauce, Polenta with Shrimp
    and, 59
Sausage and Black Bean Soup, 172
Sausage Soup, Hearty Chicken-, 170
Scallops and Tomatoes, Grilled, 57

Seafood. See specific types and Fish.
Shrimp
   Fettuccine and Shrimp, Zesty, 60
   Gazpacho, Chunky Shrimp, 165
   Polenta with Shrimp and Tomato
     Sauce, 59
   Sweet-and-Sour Shrimp, 58
Slaws
   Honey-Kissed Slaw, 132
   Veggie Slaw, Quick, 133
   Zesty Coleslaw, 133
Slow Cooker
   Chicken and Barley, Fruited, 114
   Chicken and Lentils, Moroccan, 112
   Chicken Pepper Pot, 113
   Chili Grande, 167
   Soup, Hearty Chicken-
     Sausage, 170
   Stew, Mediterranean Beef, 168
   Turkey, Glazed, 127
Snacks
   Chips, Bagel, 15
   Chips, Toasted Pita, 16
   Crisps, Baked Won Ton, 18
   Crisps, Cinnamon Waffle, 18
   Wedges, Tortilla, 17
   Wedges, Zesty Pita, 16
Soups. See also Chili, Gazpacho,
   Stew.
   Chicken-Sausage Soup,
     Hearty, 170
   Chicken-Spinach Soup,
     Creamy, 169
   Potato Soup, Roasted Garlic-, 162
   Sausage and Black Bean
     Soup, 172
   Tomato-Cheese Ravioli Soup, 164
   Turkey-Vegetable Soup, 171
   Vegetable Soup, Creamy, 163
Spinach
   Grouper Athenian, 47
   Salad, Couscous, 142
   Salad, Spinach-Onion, 137
   Salad, Sweet-and-Sour
     Spinach, 138
   Soup, Creamy Chicken-
     Spinach, 169
   Tortellini with Kidney Beans,
     Spinach, 143
   Wilted Spinach, Honey-Mustard
     Pork with, 95
Squash. See also Zucchini.
   Summer Squash Medley, 184
   Summer Squash over Polenta, 78
Stew. Mediterranean Beef, 168

Stir-Fry
   Beef Stir-Fry with Oyster Sauce, 90
   Chicken and Vegetables,
     Szechuan, 110
   Shrimp, Sweet-and-Sour, 58
Strawberries
   Cream, Berries and, 28
   Cream, Strawberries and, 25
   Parfaits, Strawberry Whip, 33
   Shortcakes, Strawberry, 35
   Shortcakes, Strawberry-Waffle, 32
   Sundaes, Neapolitan, 30
   Sundaes, Strawberry, 29
Stroganoff, Ground Beef, 86
Sweet-and-Sour Shrimp, 58
Sweet-and-Sour Spinach Salad, 138
Sweet Potatoes, Brown Sugar, 184

Taco Chicken Tortilla Wraps, 158
Tacos, Vegetarian, 70
Tomatoes
   Beans and Tomatoes, Skillet, 179
   Chicken Skillet, Mexican, 115
   Grilled Scallops and Tomatoes, 57
   Marinated Tomatoes, 139
   Pepper Steak, Tex-Mex, 80
   Pizza with Gorgonzola Cheese,
     Fresh Tomato, 77
   Red Snapper Vera Cruz, 51
   Salad, Balsamic Tomato, 138
   Salad, Bok Choy and Tomato, 132
   Salad, Romaine and Tomato, 135
   Salad, White Bean and Tomato, 141
   Sauce, Polenta with Shrimp and
     Tomato, 59
   Soup, Tomato-Cheese Ravioli, 164
Tortillas
   Bowls, Tortilla, 17
   Quesadillas, Speedy, 66
   Wedges, Tortilla, 17
   Wraps, Asian Chicken, 152
   Wraps, Taco Chicken Tortilla, 158
Tuna
   Pasta Primavera, Tuna, 53
   Salad, Lemony Bean and Tuna, 143
   Steaks with Salsa, Tuna, 54
Turkey
   Casserole, Mexicali Turkey
     Skillet, 124
   Glazed Turkey, 127
   Glazed Turkey with Cranberry Rice,
     Orange-, 126
   Melts, Cranberry-Turkey, 160
   Parmesan, Turkey, 125

Pepperoni Pizza, Turkey, 128
Sandwiches, Turkey Barbecue, 157
Soup, Turkey-Vegetable, 171

Vegetables. See also specific types.
   Bake, Southwestern Vegetable, 68
   Chicken and Vegetables,
     Szechuan, 110
   Chicken Cacciatore, Speedy, 116
   Chili Grande, 167
   Crudités, Vegetable, 186
   Gazpacho, Chunky Shrimp, 165
   Omelet, Confetti Cheese, 71
   Panini with Feta, Vegetable, 146
   Primavera, Tuna Pasta, 53
   Primavera with Pesto Sauce,
     Tortellini, 74
   Skillet Ziti and Vegetables, 75
   Slaw, Quick Veggie, 133
   Soup, Creamy Vegetable, 163
   Soup, Turkey-Vegetable, 171
   Stew, Mediterranean Beef, 168
   Tacos, Vegetarian, 70
   Wraps, Asian Chicken, 152

Waffles
   Crisps, Cinnamon Waffle, 18
   Fruit Cup, Layered Waffle-, 29
   Shortcakes, Strawberry-Waffle, 32
   Wafflewiches, 32
Walnuts, Curried Couscous
   with, 187
Won Ton Crisps, Baked, 18

Yogurt
   Berries and Cream, 28
   Cinnamon-Apple Yogurt, 26
   Frozen Yogurt, Chocolate
     Chip, 25
   Frozen Yogurt, Fruited, 28
   Smoothies, Raspberry, 27
   Sundaes, Honeybee, 27
   Sundaes, Neapolitan, 30
   Sundaes, Strawberry, 29
   Wafflewiches, 32

Zucchini
   Medley, Summer Squash, 184
   Pasta with Zucchini,
     Mediterranean, 73
   Skillet Zucchini, 185
   Sticks, Zucchini, 185

Microwave Cooking Chart for Vegetables

Cooking vegetables in the microwave is the best way to preserve nutrients and flavor, and often the quickest way to cook them. Cook all the vegetables at HIGH power in a baking dish covered with wax paper. If you use plastic wrap to cover the dish, be sure to turn back one corner to allow steam to escape.

Food	Microwave Cooking Time	Special Instructions
Asparagus, 1 pound	6 to 7 minutes	Add ¼ cup water
Beans, green, 1 pound	14 to 15 minutes	Add ½ cup water
Broccoli spears, 1 pound	7 to 8 minutes	Arrange in a circle, spoke-fashion, with flowerets in center; add ½ cup water
Carrot slices, 1 pound	9 to 10 minutes; stand 2 minutes	Add ¼ cup water
Cauliflower flowerets, 1 pound	7 to 8 minutes; stand 2 minutes	Add ¼ cup water
Corn on the cob, 2 (large) ears 3 ears 4 ears	5 to 9 minutes 7 to 12 minutes 8 to 15 minutes	Arrange end-to-end in a circle; add ¼ cup water
Onions, peeled and quartered, 1 pound	6 to 8 minutes	Add 2 tablespoons water
Peas, green, shelled, 1 pound (about 1½ cups)	6 to 7 minutes	Add 2 tablespoons water
Potatoes, baking/sweet, medium 1 potato 2 potatoes 4 potatoes	4 to 6 minutes 7 to 8 minutes 12 to 14 minutes	Pierce skins and arrange end-to-end in a circle; let stand 5 minutes after cooking
New potatoes, 1 pound	8 to 10 minutes	Pierce if unpeeled; add ¼ cup water
Spinach, 10-ounce package fresh leaves	2 to 3 minutes	Wash leaves before cooking
Squash, Yellow/Zucchini, 1 pound, sliced (4 medium)	7 to 8 minutes	Add ¼ cup water
Squash, Acorn, 2 pounds, (2 medium)	9 to 10 minutes	Pierce skins
Turnips, 1¼ pounds, peeled and cubed (4 medium)	10 to 12 minutes	Add ¼ cup water